Thank you for you

Lord continue to

for his glory! v inc 1.6

S M Davis

"Written from a Protestant perspective, Stephen Davis brilliantly chronicles the centuries-long Huguenot fight for survival and legal recognition in France from the earliest days of the Reformation to the 1905 Law of Separation of Church and State. The book colorfully describes religious persecution, wars, massacres, revolutions, and how the Protestants survived against long odds."

—MARTIN I. KLAUBER, affiliate professor of church history,
    Trinity Evangelical Divinity School

"Stephen Davis has, again, brought the plight of the French Protestant to life in this rich, scholarly, and penetrating analysis. The success of the German, Swiss, and English Reformations tend to result in a lack of interest in what was transpiring in France, but Davis helps to recalibrate our focus by exploring the challenges faced by the French Protestants. I heartily encourage any student of the Reformation to enrich their knowledge through this book."

—TK DUNN, associate professor of history and theology,
    Columbia International University

"This clearly written and balanced overview of Protestantism in France from 1517 to 1905 covers the Reformation, era of religious wars, and the Revolution, but also the less familiar—and more positive—developments for them during the Republics, the Napoleonic Era, and the Dreyfus Affair. Until a 1905 law ended the Catholic Church's official power by separating church and state, Protestants in France demonstrated remarkable resilience."

—DOUGLAS CARL ABRAMS, author of *Missionaries in the Golden Age of Hollywood*

"Stephen Davis's book is a valuable look at the long history of French Protestantism. Previous works have addressed Protestantism in France up to the time of the Revocation of the Edict of Nantes, but Davis continues the story through the French Revolution into the twentieth century. Davis helps the reader better understand the ways in which Protestants negotiated religious and political upheavals for almost four hundred years and provides practical insights for Christians facing persecution in the twenty-first century."

  —MARK DRAPER, associate professor of church history,
   Lancaster Bible College

French Protestantism's Struggle for Survival and Legitimacy

1517–1905

French Protestantism's Struggle for Survival and Legitimacy

1517–1905

STEPHEN M. DAVIS

WIPF & STOCK · Eugene, Oregon

FRENCH PROTESTANTISM'S STRUGGLE FOR SURVIVAL AND
LEGITIMACY (1517–1905)

Wipf & Stock
An Imprint of Wipf and Stock Publishers
199 W. 8th Ave., Suite 3
Eugene, OR 97401

www.wipfandstock.com

PAPERBACK ISBN: 978-1-6667-7131-2
HARDCOVER ISBN: 978-1-6667-7132-9
EBOOK ISBN: 978-1-6667-7133-6

Contents

CONTENTS

Preface

MY LOVE FOR THE French language and people began when my family lived in France in the late 1980s and early 1990s. My admiration and appreciation have grown for the history of French Protestantism and the struggles of Protestants to survive as a minority in a hostile political and religious climate. This book highlights some of the main events and persons in the history of French Protestantism beginning with the sixteenth-century Protestant Reformation and ending with the Law of Separation of Church and State in 1905. Several of the chapters first appeared online at *World History Encyclopedia* and are used with permission. Some material is borrowed and edited from two books I have written on French history: *Rise of French Laïcité* and *The French Huguenots and Wars of Religion.*

There were two main branches of the Protestant Reformation in France—Reformed and Lutheran—which followed the teachings of the Frenchman John Calvin and the German Martin Luther respectively. Luther's teachings initially received an enthusiastic reception in several regions of France. Once Calvin appeared on the scene, his teachings had a greater impact throughout France in both the number of followers and influence. Lutherans followed the Confession of Augsburg (1530). Reformed Protestants adhered to the Confession of Faith written by Calvin (1559). The emphasis in this book is the history of French Reformed Protestantism since it is recognized that Lutheran Protestants in Alsace did not experience the same history as the rest of France.[1] There are, however, references to Lutheranism due to its early influence in France. Lutherans were concentrated in the eastern regions of Alsace-Lorraine which bordered Germany. These regions were part of France beginning with Louis XIV, annexed by Germany after France's defeat in the Franco-Prussian War (1870–1871), and returned to France in 1918 as part of the Treaty of Versailles after Germany's defeat in WWI.

1. Encrevé, *Les protestants*, §11,409.

Introduction

AT THE DAWN OF the Protestant Reformation, French Protestants began their struggle for legitimacy, religious equality, and civil rights.[1] They faced opposition from the monarchy and the state religion, the Roman Catholic Church. For centuries the Catholic Church had influenced every aspect of life—cultural, educational, social, political, and economic. The nation and culture were thoroughly Catholic. Protestantism arrived as a foreign invader and disrupted the Catholic monopoly. A civil war was inevitable and bloodied France for decades. To end the Wars of Religion (1562–1598), Henry IV (r. 1589–1610)[2] promulgated the Edict of Nantes in 1598 protecting Protestantism. His grandson Louis XIV (r. 1643–1715) revoked the edict in 1685 resulting in the War of the Camisards (1702–1705). With the Edict of Toleration in 1787 under Louis XVI (r. 1774–1792), French Protestants were granted civil rights and permitted to practice their religion privately in the kingdom without the threat of persecution. The legal rights obtained by Protestants did not always translate into protection from violence and discrimination. Protestantism was

1. According to Stéphan, the term "Protestant" was not employed widely in France until the seventeenth century and non-Lutheran, Reformed believers were called Huguenots (*L'Épopée huguenote*, 65). The terms "Protestant," "Reformed," "Calvinist," and "Huguenot" are used interchangeably by French authors to describe non-Catholic believers who identified with the teaching of John Calvin.

2. For dates in parentheses: "r." indicates years of reign for kings and emperors, "p." marks the beginning and end of a pope's papacy, and "l." indicates the year of birth and death for all other individuals.

tolerated but did not have equal standing with the state religion, and non-Catholics remained excluded from employment in education and public service.

At the opening of the French Revolution in 1789, the Declaration of the Rights of Man and of the Citizen announced a new era of religious tolerance and permitted greater access to employment and military positions for non-Catholics. Article ten stated, "No one may be disturbed on account of his opinions, even religious ones, as long as the manifestation of such opinions does not interfere with the established Law and Order." For a time, this masterful and ground-breaking statement remained an ideal yet served as a reference point and foundation for changes to come. The century following the Revolution marked French Protestantism with two major events: 1) The Concordat and Organic Articles under Napoleon; 2) A theological crisis that divided Protestantism into two factions—evangelical/orthodox Protestants who affirmed the fundamentals of Christianity as formulated by the Reformers and liberal Protestants who questioned or denied them. One of the central issues championed by orthodox leaders was the necessity of a confession of faith for churches and ministers of the French Reformed Church.

French Protestants found a greater measure of protection of religious rights with the Concordat of 1801 and the Organic Articles in 1802 under Napoleon Bonaparte (l. 1769–1821). The Concordat with the Vatican defined France's relationship with the Catholic Church for over one hundred years. Catholicism was no longer the state religion but the religion of the majority of French people. The Organic Articles were added in 1802 and provided state recognition of the Reformed and Lutheran confessions alongside the Catholic Church. During the nineteenth century, political upheaval and attempts to reestablish Catholicism as the state religion led to the termination of the Concordat in 1905 except in the region of Alsace-Lorraine for historical reasons. The Law of Separation of Church and State in 1905 ended state recognition of any religious confession, ensured freedom of conscience, declared state neutrality in religious matters, ended the struggle between a secular Republic and the Catholic Church, and provided a legal framework for freedom of worship.

The twenty-first century presents some interesting parallels with French history which might help Americans better understand current challenges to people of faith in their context. I do not want to exaggerate the situation of Christians in America today or try to compare it with the repression and persecution experienced by Protestants in France, or with the persecution presently experienced by Christians around the world. But I want readers to reflect on what happens when either religion or government assumes powers and roles which have not been attributed to them by the law of the land, the laws of God, or the will of citizens. Throughout the centuries, French Protestants demonstrated their loyalty to the monarchy and then to the French Republic and its values. They resisted only when the government and state church violated their consciences and their homes. Christians respect the institution of government because it is divinely ordained (Rom 13) and they are called to "render to Caesar the things that are Caesar's." They are also called to render "to God the things that are God's" (Mark 12:17). When there is a conflict between Caesar and God, Christians "must obey God rather than men" (Acts 5:29). Because of their convictions, Christians must oppose every ideology or movement that contradicts what God has divinely revealed in his word. Or as the Apostle Paul stated, "We destroy arguments and every lofty opinion raised against the knowledge of God, and take every thought captive to obey Christ" (2 Cor 10:5).

CHAPTER 1

Protestant Reformation
in Sixteenth-Century France

THE PROTESTANT REFORMATION OF the sixteenth century began a period of social, political, and religious turmoil in Europe that would destabilize nations and disrupt the religious monopoly held by the Roman Catholic Church. One nineteenth-century French historian claimed that the Reformation was the greatest event of modern times and marked the starting point for a new world.[1] For centuries popes claimed to represent Jesus Christ as the Vicar of Christ on earth, and the decrees of popes were placed on the same level of authority as Holy Scripture. The Catholic Church's "immense structure was nothing less than the City of God. Generation upon generation of Christians laboured to build it."[2]

The Church served as a unifying factor in Europe against invasions from the East. And although the Church never denied the fundamental truths of Christianity—the Trinity, the deity and virgin birth of Christ, his sacrificial death on the cross, and his bodily resurrection—a whole system of traditions and dogma erased the gospel's simplicity and denied the sinner's justification by grace through faith alone. There were additions to the truth revealed in the Bible—saints, festivals, rituals, incense, priesthood, pilgrimages, holy water, holy places, indulgences—and the claim that there

1. Félice, *Histoire des Protestants* (1), 7.
2. Holland, *Dominion*, 312.

was no salvation apart from and outside the Church. Neither was there any assurance of salvation in a man-made religious system where one never knew if enough was done to merit the grace of God. Here and there were found individuals in monasteries, convents, and homes who sought and found the truth through the veils that obscured it. They came under suspicion and the Church's response to the challenges of its authority was the charge of heresy and the use of secular authorities to punish heretics to save their souls.[3]

Pope Gregory VII

To understand how the Protestant Reformation took root in European nations, we must go back to the eleventh century. Pope Gregory VII (p. 1073–1085) shook the foundations of the Christian world when he declared the authority to depose emperors. Before this time, no pope had ever challenged imperial power with such directness. In 1076 Gregory excommunicated Henry IV (r. 1084–1106), emperor of the Holy Roman Empire, the heir of Constantine and Charlemagne. Gregory began a reformation to root out corruption in the Church and advance the agenda of the papacy in laying claim to the sole leadership of the Christian people.[4]

3. Félice, *Histoire des Protestants* (1), 10.

4. Holland, *Dominion*, 227–29.

Henry IV, Holy Roman Emperor

During this period of Rome's expansion, Europe endured disaster after disaster. Troubled by the prospect of death and final judgment, people turned to the Church and her saints for protection. The dogma of purgatory was conceived as an intermediate place between heaven and hell and led the Church to offer indulgences to shorten the period of suffering. The sale of indulgences did more to hasten the demise of the Catholic Church than anything else. Nothing irritated and enraged the people more than finding in their religion less morality than they found in themselves.[5] The sale of indulgences by the Dominican monk Johann Tetzel in Germany provoked Luther's indignation. Luther

5. Félice, *Histoire des Protestants* (1), 11.

protested by posting Ninety-Five Theses on the door of the Castle Church in Wittenberg on October 31, 1517. He condemned the corruption of the Roman Catholic Church, insisted on the authority of Scripture and justification by faith alone, and sparked the Protestant Reformation.

Luther's 95 Theses

Attempts at reform from within the Catholic Church targeted the clergy and religious life. Those who called for reform denounced the abuses of the clergy and the accumulation of privileges at all levels of the hierarchical ladder. Mystics during the Middle Ages like Bernard of Clairvaux (l. 1090–1153) and Nicholas of Clémangis (l. 1363–1437) sought to renew the Church in their times and failed because they never attacked the root of the evil.[6] As a faithful Catholic monk, Luther initially sought the reform of the Church from within. In time he understood the Church's intransigence and the impossibility of doctrinal reform.[7] The Council of Trent (1545–1563) mounted a Counter-Reformation to condemn the Protestant Reformation, establish Catholic dogma and attempt a reform of the pervasive moral laxity and indiscipline among the clergy, a reform of morals but not of doctrine.[8] The thirty-two

6. Félice, *Histoire des Protestants* (1), 13–14.

7. Bost, *Histoire des Protestants*, 28.

8. See Lehner, *Catholic Reform*, for a Catholic view of differences between

canons of the council demonstrate the gap between Catholic and Reformation theology regarding justification by faith. Catholic theology rightly asserts that justification is a gift of God but wrongly affirms that "as long as you remain in the faith and keep doing the works, then you remain in justification" and "if you do not do the works, that is, you sin, then you lose your justification."[9] Catholic justification must be sustained by works, can be lost by sin, and then regained upon repentance and a return to the grace of God. Reformation teaching "diverged from Rome not only in affirming that faith alone justifies, but also in defining the faith that justifies in the way that it did."[10] Protestants understand that in justification God declares that one is righteous by faith alone through Christ alone and that good works follow faith (Eph 2:10).

TIME OF REFORMATION

After centuries of the Catholic Church's monopoly, why did the Reformation occur then? From a divine perspective, it was God's time. Yet we cannot ignore human and historical factors. There was a widespread spiritual crisis throughout Europe with multiple causes. Above all, at the root of the spiritual crisis was the Church's "total inability to bring peace and solace to troubled generations in an era of dissolving certainties."[11] The emergence of a religious minority in a kingdom of Catholic religion and culture led to confessional and political confrontation. In a few decades, the Reformation's influence in France "not only shattered the unity of religion, but it led to the contesting of the monarchy itself."[12]

The Church in Western Europe during the Middle Ages also experienced a fragile unity. There were schisms, notably that of the Eastern Church in the eleventh century. Competing popes with

---

Catholic Reform and Protestant Reformation, 2.

9. Ryan and Horton, *Justified*, 59.

10. Ryan and Horton, *Justified*, 47.

11. Elton, *Reformation Europe*, 11.

12. Holt, "Kingdom of France," 23.

rival claims for the papal throne during the fourteenth century produced a crisis of authority and damaged the Church's prestige. For centuries the Inquisition was a powerful tool of the Church to combat pre-Reformation reformers. The Spanish inquisitor Tomàs de Torquemada allegedly burned over 8,000 people and tortured another 90,000 for various crimes.[13] Through the relentless efforts of the Inquisition, those sects considered the most dangerous, the Cathars and Albigensians, largely disappeared by the fourteenth century. The Waldensians endured and suffered further persecution during the sixteenth century (chapter 3). The Congregation of the Holy Office was instituted in 1542 by Pope Paul III (p. 1534–1549) "with the purpose of defending and upholding Catholic faith and morals. One of its specific duties was to take over the suppression of heresies and heretics which had been handled by the Medieval Inquisition."[14] The Protestant Reformation swept across Europe accompanied by violence and transformation on an unprecedented scale. Luther's early writings were eagerly received in France before their condemnation by the Sorbonne in 1521. His writings spread so widely that they were soon censured and publicly burned. Beginning in 1523 those who embraced the new teachings were pursued and many were put to death as heretics.[15]

Before the Wars of Religion (1562–1598), there was little organized Protestant resistance to the State. The preaching of the gospel and the death of martyrs were persuasive in themselves and multitudes were won to the new faith. Many who embraced the teachings of Luther worked for reform within the Church. Others went further and adopted a new religion which placed them in opposition to the established political and ecclesiastical powers. The Holy Roman Empire fought with a vengeance against those who challenged its centuries-old authority and domination. The Reformation in France "was more enthusiastically received in the poorer provinces (parts of Languedoc and the Dauphiné)" and "was more firmly established in those provinces which enjoyed

13. Moorhead, *Trial of the 16th Century*, 26n.

14. Finocchiaro, *On Trial for Reason*, 21.

15. Elton, *Reformation Europe*, 81.

the most independence of royal authority . . . Brittany, Navarre, and Guyenne."[16]

REFORMERS

Martin Luther and John Calvin are the two most well-known Reformers. The influence of their pamphlets and books was such that in 1535 King Francis I ordered the closure of all printshops in the kingdom of France. There were other Reformers—Theodore Beza (l. 1519–1605) ministered alongside Calvin; William Farel (l.1489–1565) fled to Switzerland in 1530 to escape persecution; Philip Melanchthon (l. 1497–1560) was a collaborator of Luther; Ulrich Zwingli (l. 1484–1531) led the Reformation in Switzerland and died on the field of battle. The Reformers were not bringing novel religious teaching. They sought to restore apostolic teaching by affirming the authority of the Scriptures above church traditions, councils, and papal proclamations. They asserted that salvation was found uniquely in the person of Jesus Christ and his sacrifice for sins on the cross apart from works and apart from the established Church.

The role of Gutenberg's invention of the printing press in 1450 in the propagation of Reformed teaching cannot be exaggerated. During medieval times, pamphlets and books were available only through the time-consuming and faulty method of copying. The printing press provided more security in the transmission of ideas and assured a rapid spread of the message.[17] The seditious ideas of Luther entered the French kingdom and led to waves of persecution. The Reformation continued and expanded in France under John Calvin with the publication of his *Institutes of the Christian Religion*, in Latin in 1536 and French in 1541.

---

16. Poland, *Protestantism in France*, 11–12.

17. Garrisson, *Histoire des protestants*, 23.

Martin Luther

Martin Luther

Martin Luther (l. 1483–1546) was born in Saxony, Germany, the son of a miner. At the age of twenty-two, he became a monk and entered the convent of Augustinians at Erfurt. "As a monk, Luther lived in dread of judgement, starving himself and praying every night, confessing his sins for long hours, wearying his superiors, all in a despairing attempt to render himself deserving of heaven."[18] Luther came to understand "that the corruption of the gospel in his own day had resulted in the abandonment of justification *sola*

18. Holland, *Dominion*, 318.

8

gratia and *sola fide*."[19] On October 31, 1517, after nailing his famous Ninety-Five Theses on the door of the Castle Church in Wittenberg, he was ordered by the Church to recant his error or face excommunication. Rather than recant, he burned the papal bull of excommunication outlining his supposed errors, and in 1520 he published writings against the tyranny of the papacy. The popular support Luther enjoyed and his refusal to recant threatened the stability of the Holy Roman Empire and at the same time overturned the teachings and practices of meritorious good works—indulgences, penitence, flagellations, and the veneration of saints.[20]

Charles V, Holy Roman Emperor

19. Barrett, "Crux of Genuine Reform," 46.
20. Félice, *Histoire des Protestants* (1), 17.

Summoned to the Diet of Worms called by Emperor Charles V (r. 1519–1556), Luther was promised safe passage and held at the Episcopal Palace. One historian claims that "Luther's appearance at Worms proved to be the true beginning of the Reformation."[21] On the first day of Luther's trial in April 1521, Johann Eck asked him to renounce the errors in his published works. Luther requested a day for reflection and reappeared the next day to express his conviction of the ultimate authority of the word of God to which he would submit. In defiance before German princes, bishops, and lords, Luther proclaimed that he would only be persuaded by Holy Scriptures and would not violate his conscience, bound by the Scriptures.

Luther married Katharina von Bora (l. 1499–1552) in 1525. She and other nuns had escaped their convent in 1523 and joined Luther's reform movement. Luther was persuaded that if there were compelling reasons to forbid priests to marry, there were stronger reasons to allow marriage.[22] Among his many accomplishments, Luther translated the Greek New Testament into German in 1522 and the Hebrew Old Testament into German in 1534. He is credited with establishing five fundamental principles (or *solas* from the Latin): Scripture alone, faith alone, grace alone, Christ alone, to the glory of God alone. These scriptural truths set his teaching apart from the teaching of the Catholic Church and prefigured an inevitable rupture. Luther's influence in France would soon be eclipsed by that of Calvin, but Luther's influence was undeniable as a catalyst for the Reformation.[23] Without question, "his dogmatic departure from the Roman Catholic Church . . . fundamentally transformed European society at every level."[24]

Although Luther came to clearly understand the gospel of justification by faith alone, his views of religious freedom are complex and at times appear contradictory. Some historians argue that

---

21. Elton, *Reformation Europe*, 27.

22. Félice, *Histoire des Protestants* (1), 18.

23. Elton, *Reformation Europe*, 3.

24. Higdon, "Martin Luther," 422.

"Luther endorsed the use of the civil sword in order to suppress false teachers."[25] His teaching on the relationship between church and state was complicated by the Peasants' War (1524–1525) and the role of the State in suppressing heretics whose teachings led to rebellion and insurrection. His political theology oscillated throughout his life, yet Luther "continued to place his support behind some level of religious tolerance."[26] The boundaries between church and state were not always clear as the Reformers implemented their vision of a Christian society. Some Reformers, who believed in protecting an established church, held that "ecclesial schism was equated with civil rebellion and sedition."[27] At times, Protestants repeated the error of the Catholic Church in their intolerance toward dissidents, and they established state religions in other nations. In England, the Protestant Queen Elizabeth I (r. 1558–1603) "employed one of the most brutal execution devices of all time: being drawn, hung and quartered."[28] In France, however, Protestants never reached a critical mass with enough influence to establish a state religion and there is probably no way of knowing if they would have done so given the right circumstances.

25. Higdon, "Martin Luther," 416.
26. Higdon, "Martin Luther," 425.
27. Higdon, "Martin Luther," 429.
28. Moorhead, *Trial of the 16th Century*, 26.

John Calvin

John Calvin

John Calvin (l. 1509–1564) was born in Noyon, France in the region of Picardy. At the age of fourteen, he attended the University of Paris and then transferred to the Collège de Montaigu to study liberal arts.[29] He received a classical education through which he acquired an encyclopedic knowledge of authors from antiquity and the patristic period. He later studied law until the death of his father in 1531.[30] The exact time of his conversion is debated but around 1533 there was a radical change in his life. A Bible given to him by one of his relatives released him from captivity to Catholicism. He was charged with heresy by the Sorbonne and forced to flee. Under an assumed name, Charles d'Espeville, he found refuge at Angoulême where he continued the work begun on the *Institutes of the Christian Religion*, the first theological and literary monument of the Reformation. He preached Reformed doctrine in the regions of Poitou and Saintonge, publicly when able, and

29. McKim, *John Calvin*, 3.

30. Bloch, *Réforme Protestante*, 14.

secretly when the persecution became violent. Constantly in danger, he left France for Basel, Switzerland where he completed the *Institutes*. In the preface to his commentary on the Psalms, Calvin explained the reason for the *Institutes*—to remove the unjust accusations against his brothers whose deaths were precious in God's eyes. The first edition of his *Institutes* in Latin was dedicated to the French king and became the standard exposition of Reformation teaching.[31] In the preface, Calvin once again came to the defense of those unjustly persecuted and laid the blame on the tyranny of his adversaries rather than on the king himself.[32]

In 1536, Calvin passed through Geneva where Farel needed help in organizing a new church. Geneva was a refuge for French Protestants and Calvin organized them into the first French Reformed church. In this early period, "Calvin was little more than a minor civil servant, living in the city under suffrance. It was the city council—not Calvin, Farel, or Viret—who controlled the religious affairs of the new republic."[33] Both Calvin and Farel were briefly chased from Geneva in 1538 due to religious laws Farel sought to impose on the city. Among the laws was a requirement that all inhabitants of Geneva affirm their allegiance to Calvin's Confession of Faith.[34] Calvin went to Strasbourg where he met the Reformer Martin Bucer (l. 1491–1551). The French Reformation found early support in Strasbourg, later reinforced in Geneva. It was in Strasbourg that Calvin began writing his *Commentaries on the Bible*. Doctrines that became known as Calvinism were spread throughout Europe and beyond. Calvin called upon believers living in places with no Protestant church to separate from the Catholic Church, and if necessary, relocate to a place where they could worship freely.[35]

Calvin returned to Geneva in 1541 where he ministered for twenty-three more years. Citizenship in Geneva was reserved for

31. Félice, *Histoire des Protestants* (1), 50–52.
32. Calvin, *L'Institution Chrétienne*, XXII–XXV.
33. McGrath, *Life of John Calvin*, 98.
34. McGrath, *Life of John Calvin*, 99.
35. Bost, *Histoire des Protestants*, 45.

native-born residents and Calvin was unable to become a citizen or vote in elections. Thus, "his influence over Geneva was exercised indirectly, through preaching, consultation, and other forms of legitimate suasion."[36] His ministry was often in jeopardy to the point where he believed he would be expelled from the city. He and other pastors were opposed by magistrates over "who had the authority to ban someone from partaking of the Lord's Supper.[37] English exiles in 1555 effusively described what they saw in Geneva as "the very model of a Christian commonwealth: a society in which freedom and discipline were so perfectly in balance that none of them would ever forget the experience."[38] Some might question that assessment in light of the execution of Michael Servetus in 1553 which is "one of the most debated events in the life of John Calvin . . . , unfortunately, the retelling of the story is often dependent on the historian's relationship to Calvinism."[39] Calvin did not vote on Servetus' sentence and "made an appeal for a less barbarous form of execution."[40] It seems clear, however, that Calvin supported the magistrates' decision to execute Servetus. We must keep in mind that since "execution for heresy was acceptable at the time (it was Imperial law), that it was practiced among the major Protestant cities, and that the killing of Servetus was approved of by major Protestant theologians, it should give serious pause to anyone who would single out Calvin for condemnation."[41] Calvin was a child of his time, as we are of ours, and although his approval of the execution cannot be ignored, "each time period must be judged by the prevailing laws of the time, not those of the future."[42] Yet it should not be denied that although to a lesser degree than

36. McGrath, *Life of John Calvin*, 109.

37. Moorhead, *Trial of the 16th Century*, 53.

38. Holland, *Dominion*, 329–30.

39. Moorhead, *Trial of the 16th Century*, 8.

40. Moorhead, *Trial of the 16th Century*, 77.

41. Moorhead, *Trial of the 16th Century*, 89.

42. Moorhead, *Trial of the 16th Century*, 91.

the Catholic Church, Protestants wielding political power also engaged in persecution and participated in executions.[43]

The first synod of the Reformed church took place in 1559 which laid the foundation for the French Reformation with a confession of faith and constitution written by Calvin. At the time of his death in 1564, his contemporaries reported that he died poor, and apart from his library left few possessions. This testimony moved one skeptic to admire Calvin's virtue and the power of his life as a minister of the gospel.[44] Believers known as Calvinists "would prove themselves ready to follow his teachings even at the utmost cost: to abandon their past; to leave behind their homes; to travel, if they had to, to the ends of the earth."[45]

CONCLUSION

The arrival of the Reformation in Europe with its emphasis on 1) the authority of Scripture, 2) the priesthood of the believer, and 3) the freedom of conscience undermined the Catholic Church's grip on European society. The Reformation, in the measure that it brought back religion and Christian churches to the purity of their origins according to the intention of the Reformers, marked the beginning of the restoration of the principles of freedom of conscience and worship, and at the same time, the separation of powers—civil and ecclesiastical.[46] Five hundred years later, the Reformation's historical and religious importance cannot be exaggerated. It is unarguable that the Reformation changed the course of history not only in Western Europe but throughout the world.

In light of the suffering and bloodshed associated with the Reformation, questions have been raised about the Reformation's necessity or inevitability. Many causes surely contributed to the Reformation—fear of death heightened by plagues, clergy abuses,

43. Moorhead, *Trial of the 16th Century*, 26–27.
44. Félice, *Histoire des Protestants* (1), 57.
45. Holland, *Dominion*, 332.
46. Réveillard, *La séparation*, 23.

economic uncertainty, and Renaissance influences. Above all, "the Reformation was a theological movement, caused by doctrinal concerns."[47] The Reformation began with a biblical understanding of the doctrine of justification by faith alone. Although the "material cause" of the Reformation was justification by faith, the Reformers' "focus in communicating the gospel was not primarily justification, but Jesus Christ in whom we find our justification."[48] The decades and centuries that followed brought persecution and suffering as Protestants fought and died for these doctrinal issues and the principles of freedom of conscience and freedom of worship.

47. Barrett, "Crux of Genuine Reform," 44.
48. Ferguson, "Justification," 232.

CHAPTER 2

Reformation and Repression in Meaux

1521

AS THE PROTESTANT REFORMATION DEVELOPED IN France in the early sixteenth century, the city of Meaux, twenty-five miles east of Paris, became one of the first centers of controversy. Bishop Guillaume Briçonnet II (l. 1472–1534) undertook a campaign to reform the Catholic Church from within and called Jacques Lefèvre, a leading figure in French humanism, to lead missionary efforts along with William Farel. Soon all three found themselves at odds with the Catholic hierarchy.

Bishop Guillaume Briçonnet

REFORMATION IN THE CATHOLIC CHURCH

Statue of William Farel at Neuenberg

Until the sixteenth century, local reform movements and peasant revolts were easily suppressed. The Inquisition, instituted in
1231 by Pope Gregory IX (p. 1227–1241), had largely succeeded in
stamping out heresy. After Luther's protest in Wittenberg in 1517
against indulgences, his teachings circulated widely in France. In
the city of Meaux, Farel and the Leclerc brothers contested the veneration of Mary and the saints. They provoked the ire of the Faculty
of Theology at the Sorbonne in Paris and drew growing hostility
from parliamentarians. Farel was considered especially dangerous
because of his opposition to the dogma of purgatory. Those who
embraced these new teachings were often called Lutherans even if

they had little contact with the German Reformation; Lutherans were anyone suspected of heresy.[1]

Guillaume Briçonnet II was made bishop of Lodève in 1489 at the age of seventeen and followed in the steps of his father, Cardinal Briçonnet (l. 1445–1514). His father left Rome in 1510 with four other cardinals to launch reforms in the Church in opposition to Pope Julius II (p. 1503–1513). Shortly after King Francis I's enthronement (r. 1515–1547), he sent Briçonnet II to Rome to negotiate the Concordat of Bologna (1516) with Pope Leo X (p. 1513–1521). The Concordat removed the French Church's traditional rights of election and granted the king the authority to make appointments to major ecclesiastical positions. Both the high clergy and nobility were placed under the king's control. The king was able to reward his most faithful servants by offering them abbeys, bishoprics, titles, and other benefits. The Concordat encountered opposition and might have pushed some clergy toward the Reformation because of questionable appointments. Yet the Concordat accomplished Francis I's aim to attach French royalty to the Catholic Church and guaranteed a Catholic monarchy.[2]

Bishop Briçonnet II entered Meaux in 1516 with great concern for the ecclesiastical problems of the Church. He became a confidant of Francis I whose religious positions fluctuated between his counselors and his sister Marguerite of Navarre (l. 1492–1549), the grandmother of the future King Henry IV and sympathetic to Reformed teaching. Catholic priests presented the new religion as the enemy of social order in the kingdom and an attack on the divine right of the monarchy. Francis I viewed the Reformation as a war machine against the monks he disdained.[3]

---

1. Miquel, *Guerres de religion*, 10.
2. Stéphan, *L'Épopée huguenote*, 35–36.
3. Félice, *Histoire des Protestants* (1), 43.

19

King Francis I of France

Briçonnet inherited a bishopric similar to many others in France. People panicked at the thought of dying without the last rites, and there was little knowledge of the Holy Scriptures among the peasantry. The Virgin was solicited for all their needs, each saint had its specialty, and sacred relics imported from the Holy Land after the crusades were treated as talismans. Most of the priests lived in Paris off the revenues from their lands in Meaux and the tithes of the faithful. They sent vicars with little training or authority to minister in their absence. During the festivals, monks preached from parish to parish more concerned about filling their pockets than edifying the faithful. The new bishop took note of these deficiencies in his diocese and set out to correct them. One of his first steps was to require Paris priests to live in their residences in Meaux.[4] In 1518, he hired preachers and sent them throughout

4. Félice, *Histoire des Protestants* (1), 27.

his parishes to evangelize Catholics who had fallen away from the Church in their commitment to religious observances. A year later, with discouraging results, Briçonnet decided to train new priests and pursue his project of reform. He held the conviction that the reformation of customs and mores was useless apart from a transformation of the inner person. To that end, he turned to Jacques Lefèvre d'Étaples from Picardy.[5]

Lefèvre d'Étaples

Lefèvre d'Étaples (l. 1450–1537) taught philosophy at the University of Paris from 1490 to 1508 where he first came into contact with the Briçonnet family. He was known for his extreme religious devotion in attending the Mass and processions and praying for hours at the feet of statues of Mary. Through reading the Bible in 1512, his eyes were opened to the biblical truth of justification by faith. The date of his new understanding of justification serves as a

5. Miquel, *Guerres de religion*, 40–46.

reminder that God was at work in different places and times before Luther came on the scene.[6] Bishop Briçonnet II invited Lefèvre to Meaux in 1521 to spearhead reformation initiatives within the Catholic Church. As a result of Lefèvre's activities and teaching, Meaux became the principal place of activity for the "evangelicals" and a group known as the Circle of Meaux. Lefèvre was passionate about bringing the Scriptures to everyone in their language. In the eyes of some, however, he appeared factious and dangerous and was surveilled by his adversaries. He raised the question on which all future Reformers would take a position—the relationship between faith and works in the justification of sinners. Lefèvre exhorted Christians to read and meditate on the Gospels and opposed the Church's position that commoners could never sound the sublime depths of Scripture.[7]

On this essential point, the Catholic Church and different streams of Reformation thought radically diverged. For the Church, doctrinal truth resided in Scripture and dogmas established by tradition. For the Reformers, doctrinal truth resided in Scripture alone and every believer had the right and the duty to search and understand its truths. Although adversaries at the Faculty of Theology of Paris treated Lefèvre with contempt, the opposition did not stop Parisian students from visiting Meaux.[8] There were other notable visitors at Meaux such as Marguerite and her queen mother, Louise of Savoy. Marguerite later became queen of Navarre in 1527 and became known as the guardian angel of the evangelicals. Her poetry testifies to her spiritual sensitivity and was accompanied by her charitable works. She ardently desired the reform of the Church she loved. Even when criticized by the Faculty of Theology, she guarded the hope of a reform wrought at the interior of the Church.[9]

6. Félice, *Histoire des Protestants* (1), 25.

7. Garrisson, *Histoire des protestants*, 33.

8. Stéphan, *L'Épopée huguenote*, 36–37.

9. Stéphan, *L'Épopée huguenote*, 27–31.

Marguerite of Navarre

Despite impediments from the Faculty of Theology, and under royal protection by Marguerite, the writings of Lefèvre were widely diffused. He and the Circle of Meaux engaged in their missionary work throughout the region. They argued for a return to apostolic teaching and denounced the veneration of saints and the sale of indulgences. Lefèvre translated and published the four Gospels in 1522 and later wrote a commentary on them. The bishop encouraged him to distribute the Gospels at no charge to the poor. Sundays and holidays were consecrated to the study of the Gospels which made their way into the fields and workshops of the region. As people took the teaching seriously there was also a reformation of morals which became evident in daily life. Day laborers from Picardy and other places who came into the region of Meaux at harvest time returned to their homes with the Gospels and the teachings they heard preached. The influence was so great that a proverb circulated in France during the first half of the sixteenth century which designated any adversaries of Rome as "heretics of Meaux."[10] Lefèvre then translated the entire New and Old Testaments into French. When Lutheran teachings were condemned by the Faculty of Theology in 1521, the school at Meaux was placed under suspicion and opened the way for an era of violence.[11]

REPRESSION BY THE CATHOLIC CHURCH

Bishop Briçonnet could not ignore the excommunication of Luther by Pope Leo X in 1521. He understood that he needed to distance himself from people and events associated with the German Reformation. He also understood that although Parliament cared little for monks and priests, they held to a fundamental principle of the State: one faith, one law, one king. Friends of Lefèvre defected and returned to the teaching of the Church. While Briçonnet did not wish to end his efforts of reform and continued his mission to print and distribute the Scriptures in French, he decided to publicly condemn Luther to avoid his own condemnation. In October 1523, to placate the Faculty of Theology, Briçonnet issued edicts that forbade the sale, possession, or reading of Luther's writings. The people of Meaux were not deterred by these repressive measures and showed even more interest in the new teachings. In response, Briçonnet's adversaries began a slanderous campaign against the bishop in 1524. Posters were hung from the cathedral and plastered on walls throughout Meaux attacking Briçonnet as a Lutheran.[12]

10. Félice, *Histoire des Protestants* (1), 28.

11. Stéphan, *L'Épopée huguenote*, 25–26.

12. Miquel, *Guerres de religion*, 55.

Pope Clement VII

In December of that same year, Briçonnet was called upon to post papal bulls from Pope Clement VII (p. 1523–1534) which included the announcement of new indulgences and a three-day fast for forgiveness. The people of Meaux ripped down the papal bulls and reviled the pope as Antichrist. The city entered into a state of rebellion against the Church and royal officials now had the pretext to justify repression. In the absence of Francis I, a prisoner of Emperor Charles V after France's defeat at the Battle of Pavia in February 1525, the first persecution was unleashed. At Meaux, Briçonnet acted in vain to calm the spirits. He instructed the priests to read prayers once again for the dead and to invoke the Virgin and saints, and he took under his protection the statues and images of saints. The warnings of the bishop were no longer respected by the people; the time of martyrs arrived and the time of revolt.[13]

Jean Leclerc, a recent convert, was condemned in 1523 for hanging a poster identifying the pope as Antichrist. He was whipped for three days at different places in Meaux and branded with a hot iron on the forehead. The following year he was arrested at Metz for destroying statues, had his right hand cut off, and suffered other tortures before being burned alive as he recited the Psalms. Jacques Pauvent, a disciple of Lefèvre, was accused of writing pamphlets against purgatory, the invocation of the Virgin and saints, and holy water. The news spread, the search for heretics intensified, and the Circle of Meaux was warned that they no longer enjoyed official protection. More arrests followed and Lefèvre fled in exile to Strasbourg. At Meaux, the rebellion continued and the stories of martyrs served as fodder for sermons. In 1528, a large crowd gathered at the cathedral and posted a counterfeit bull allegedly signed by the pope to the glory of Luther. Briçonnet was scandalized by this provocation and searched for the authors of this outrage. Eight men and women were delivered to him. Six publicly recognized their fault, were condemned, branded with the fleur-de-lys on the forehead, and led through the streets as an example. One recalcitrant, Denys de Rieux, cried aloud that the Mass was a denial of the death and passion of Christ. He was dragged through the streets on a rack before being burned alive.[14]

Briçonnet himself did not escape censure by Parliament for having permitted heresy to propagate at Meaux. Other bishops severely judged the events at Meaux and laid the blame on him. He had not protected extremists who sought to abolish the hierarchy, questioned the sacraments, and destroyed statues. Yet he was accused of having permitted the so-called Lutherans to organize and freely express their views. Bishops gathered in 1528 at the Council of Sens and demanded the condemnation and punishment of the heretics at Meaux. The absolute value of all the sacraments, the adoration of Mary and veneration of the saints, and the

13. Félice, *Histoire des Protestants* (1), 32.

14. Miquel, *Guerres de religion*, 58–59.

necessity of good works for salvation were reaffirmed. The bishops reminded the king that his predecessors had not hesitated to use the sword to exterminate heresies. This call to repression was soon answered on May 31, 1528. An anonymous, iconoclastic Parisian cut off the head of a statue of Mary with the baby Jesus in her arms. The king placed a bounty on the head of the perpetrator. The guilty person was not found. Instead, the eminent humanist Louis Berquin (l. 1490–1529) was arrested. He had already been spared three times from the Faculty of Theology's condemnation through the king's intervention. His fourth imprisonment would be different. Twelve commissioners delegated by the Parliament called on Berquin to publicly renounce his teachings and condemned him to life imprisonment. Berquin's appeal to the king fell on deaf ears. His refusal to renounce his teachings led to a sentence of death by strangulation and fire. On November 10, 1529, six hundred men escorted Berquin to the place of execution where he was burned at the stake. It was the first execution of a person of renown.[15]

The persecution intensified in 1533 when Francis I met with Pope Clement VII at Marseilles to arrange the marriage between his son, the future King Henry II with Catherine de Medici (l. 1519–1589), niece of the pope. The king sought an alliance with the papacy for the conquest of Milan. Francis returned to Paris with renewed opposition to the heretics of Meaux. Many were imprisoned and the pulpit was refused to anyone who professed the Lutheran heresy. The persecution reached a climax in 1534 in the Affair of the Placards. Posters were displayed on walls around Paris to denounce the mass as sorcery. A poster was even placed on the door leading to the king's bedchamber at the Château de Blois. From this moment on, Francis I consented to brutal measures to suppress the heretics with widespread persecution.[16] The Affair of the Placards "marked the termination of Lutheran success in France and, despite the later Calvinist explosion, the end of any hope that the Reformation might conquer that country."[17]

15. Félice, *Histoire des Protestants* (1), 33–36.

16. Félice, *Histoire des Protestants* (1), 45.

17. Elton, *Reformation Europe*, 80.

CONCLUSION

Lefèvre and Briçonnet had not been able to preserve the illusion that one could evangelize in a way that called into question the order of the kingdom or threatened the state religion. Briçonnet died in 1534 without witnessing the martyrdom of the last members of the Circle of Meaux. Lefèvre, for his part, found refuge at Nérac with Marguerite, queen of Navarre. He was too old to play an active role in the French Reformation and died in his sleep, afflicted that he had not merited the fate of those slain for the Gospel that he taught them.[18] On his tomb, we are told, his last words were inscribed: "I leave my body to the earth, my spirit to God, my possessions to the poor."[19]

18. Miquel, *Guerres de religion*, 62–63.

19. Félice, *Histoire des Protestants* (1), 37.

CHAPTER 3

Massacre of the Waldensians

1545

AFTER THE OUTBREAK OF persecution at Meaux, several episodes of severe repression preceded the Wars of Religion (1562–1598). These were times of great hardship and oppression against those who embraced Protestant teachings. One notable chapter of persecution took place in the Luberon region of France against the Waldensians (*Vaudois*), the spiritual descendants of Pierre Waldo, which led to the Mérindol massacre in 1545.

MEDIEVAL RELIGIOUS PERSECUTION

In the twelfth century, Pierre Waldo (l. 1140–1218) took a vow of poverty confirmed by Pope Alexander III (p. 1159–1181) and became the leader of a sect known as the Waldensians.[1] Waldo was among the forerunners of the Reformation who sought to purify and reform the Catholic Church from within through a return to apostolic teaching. Initially, he did not seek separation from the Catholic Church or the establishment of a new sect. In time, partly due to their emphasis on preaching the gospel in the local language, Waldo and his followers were banned from preaching

---

1. Pouzet, "Les origines lyonnaises de la secte des Vaudois," 33.

29

by Pope Lucius III (p. 1181–1185). Waldo was excommunicated at the Council of Verona in 1184, and Waldensian teaching was condemned at the Fourth Lateran Council in 1215.[2]

Statue of Pierre Waldo

Exiled from their city of Lyon, the Waldensians spread to the valleys of Dauphiné and the Alps of Piedmont, to Languedoc, and Spain. The Inquisition failed to stamp them out and many of the exiles settled in the Luberon region of southern France. Their brothers in Dauphiné had previously suffered persecution and many had fled there for safety. The Waldensians sought to live in peace in the sheltered valleys of the Luberon where they drained the swamps and cultivated lands belonging to Italian lords. It is said that people inhabiting the plains feared the Waldensians who were rumored to be sorcerers. They had spiritual leaders called

2. Leconte, *Sur les traces des vaudois*, 11–13.

uncles (*barbes*) in their language who instructed the people in the knowledge and practice of the Scriptures.[3]

Waldensians as Witches

The archbishop of Aix feared that this concentration of heretics might embrace the Reformation. Around 1530, the inquisitor Jean de Roma was sent to investigate the Waldensians. Atrocities were committed and he enriched himself through the confiscation of their possessions. As a result of this initial violence, two Waldensians, Maurel and Masson, crossed the frontier to Switzerland to confer with Reformed leaders in Geneva. They were persuaded of the need to reform their beliefs, to definitively break with superstitious practices, and were sent back with letters for their brothers in Mérindol. Only Maurel arrived home safely; Masson was arrested and burned alive at Dijon. A decisive meeting

3. Miquel, *Guerres de religion*, 119–20.

took place in Piedmont in 1532 with Waldensian leadership from different regions. Over a period of six days, William Farel, who had been exiled from Meaux, convinced them to preserve only two sacraments, baptism and the Eucharist, without the mystical sense given by the Catholic Church. Farel welcomed them to the Reformed faith with enthusiasm and called them the elder sons of the Reformation.[4] Encouraged by their new friends, the Waldensians printed Robert Olivetan's French translation of the Bible in 1535. Their adversaries were irritated to see people from all walks of life convert to what they viewed as heresy.[5]

PAPAL AND ROYAL COMPLICITY

With their integration into a larger European religious confession, the Waldensians no longer felt isolated. They welcomed all who sought refuge in their mountains, in particular former Catholic priests who were valued for their literacy. Fearing that the new religion would propagate to the papal enclave of Venaissin, Pope Clement VII offered a plenary indulgence to Waldensians who renounced their Reformed faith within two months. During the waiting period, soldiers seized women and children to forcibly convert them, and young women were abducted in the village of Cabrières-du-Comtat. Their fathers, armed with clubs and pitchforks, were no match for trained soldiers and were stopped without difficulty. The news of the abductions and armed encounters circulated throughout the village. A mob emerged leading to the death of officials in Agoult and Apt. The pope wrote King Francis I to report the violence taking place at the door of papal states. The king gave instructions to the Parliament at Aix to intervene and seven Waldensians were burned at the stake, including one *barbe*.[6]

4. Miquel, *Guerres de religion*, 121.
5. Félice, *Histoire des Protestants* (1), 60.
6. Miquel, *Guerres de religion*, 122.

The intervention of the king had the effect of pushing communities to insurrection. About six thousand men belonged to the Waldensian sect at this time, and the bishops of Sisteron, Apt, and Cavaillon feared the spread of the movement throughout Provence. Members of the sect were pursued and arrested because they denied purgatory, did not pray to the saints, and refused to tithe to the clergy. The most active Waldensians were imprisoned and some were executed. Infuriated by the actions of ecclesiastical tribunals, the Waldensians took up arms to liberate their brothers and assaulted prisons in Apt, Cavaillon, and Roussillon. The king, informed of these events, offered clemency to the heretics and the release of all prisoners on the condition that they renounce their faith within six months. Yet no one accepted his proposition and in 1538 the king ordered the arrest of heretics and the confiscation of their possessions.

Rumors and Arrests

Rumors reached the Parliament in Aix that the Waldensians were preparing for a siege and had stored stocks of powder and arms. Over one hundred Waldensians were arrested, fourteen of them from Mérindol. A judge in Apt proceeded to arrest a miller and confiscated his mill after his execution. The inhabitants of Mérindol retaliated by taking up arms, burning the mill to the ground, pillaging farms, and stealing sheep along the way. As a climate of panic reigned in Aix, more unsubstantiated rumors circulated that the Waldensians were building forts in the forests and that there were six hundred men in Mérindol armed with arquebuses, a type of long gun. The exaggerated total number swelled to eight thousand combatants. Soon after, the arrest order was given which included the seizure of pregnant women. But before it was carried out, the parliamentarians realized they had been duped by local leaders. In reality, the Mérindoliens had fled to their mountains to avoid arrest after learning that an order had been given on November 18, 1540, condemning nineteen of them to be burned at the stake in three different places—Tourves, Apt, and Aix. Houses in

Mérindol would be demolished, the area rendered uninhabitable, and their possessions confiscated.[7]

Temporary Reprieve

Farel was warned by a courier of the order and contacted Swiss and German cities to intercede diplomatically with Francis I. The king charged the governor of Piedmont, Guillaume du Ballay, to investigate the Waldensians. When he delivered a favorable report, the king suspended the order and demanded the appearance of the Waldensian elders before the Parliament within three months. On April 6, 1541, instead of sending the elders before the Parliament of Aix to renounce their faith, the Mérindoliens sent their confession of faith to the Parliament and Francis I to explain their faith in Jesus Christ and the Scriptures and to affirm their spirit of obedience to civil authorities. They were willing to submit to all laws but requested freedom to practice their faith. The unyielding parliamentarians denounced the impudence of this supplication and the reaffirmation of the Waldensians' articles of faith. The king granted another three-month delay and the Parliament sent the bishop of Cavaillon to Mérindol to receive their renunciation of heresy on the spot.[8]

After further delays and the refusal to recant their faith, the king finally resolved in March 1543 to carry out the order against Mérindol. Once again, German Protestant princes, urged by Farel and Calvin, intervened with the king. In April 1544, the Waldensians presented a petition to the king to obtain justice against those who reproached their faith with the intent to confiscate their possessions. The king was aware of the avarice of the bishops and papal legates, and also knew that the parliamentarians of Aix were not above reproach. He was also hesitant to send military forces to a far-flung province. So he decided to send three members of his council and a theologian to establish whether the Waldensians

---

7. Miquel, *Guerres de religion*, 123–24.
8. Félice, *Histoire des Protestants* (1), 61.

were heretics. If found to be heretics, they would be granted another two months to renounce their faith. The Parliament of Aix was ordered to relinquish its responsibilities to the Parliament of Grenoble. As a result, the Waldensians sensed that the king hesitated to employ force against them and would protect them from the greed of the princes of the Church. Many refugees flocked to the Waldensian valleys to find shelter from persecution. Those in Geneva even thought that they had turned back the royal power. For a time at least![9]

Vain Resistance

In December 1543 Jean Meynier, Baron d'Oppède (l. 1495–1558), replaced Chassané as president of the Parliament of Aix. He had sworn to obtain the revocation of the royal letters of pardon and was committed to the annihilation of the Waldensians. Cardinal François de Tournon (l. 1489–1562), a declared enemy of heresy, supported this course of action. The local governor confirmed the exaggerated report of Meynier that the Waldensians had a force of ten thousand armed men ready to march on Marseille. The Waldensians, with little confidence in the seigneurs of Aix and Avignon, fortified their villages, notably Cabrières. The king signed an order presented to him by counselors on January 1, 1545, that revoked the pardon he had granted. Persecution in France resumed with burning stakes at Toulouse, Bordeaux, and Grenoble. Meynier kept the text hidden from his parliamentarian colleagues while awaiting the arrival in Provence of a captain from Italy, Paulin de La Garde (l. 1498–1578), the leader of a fearsome band of roving mercenaries who had fought under Francis I. Once he arrived, the Parliament gave the order to proceed to the total eradication of the heretics.

---

9. Miquel, *Guerres de religion*, 124–27.

Massacre of the Waldensians

Paulin marched on Cabrières-d'Aygues where six hundred Waldensians had reportedly gathered. The Waldensians fled and left him wondering why he had been called to employ his army against mere villagers. The army and Parliament leaders from Aix agreed to seize the heretics and burn their houses as an example to others. Paulin's men were professional soldiers, joined by troops gathered by Meynier and by volunteers eager to profit from the plunder. The inhabitants of Mérindol fled to the Luberon forests while two hundred farms were burned. Those too weak or too old to flee were massacred. Hidden in the ravines, the villagers learned that the army had entered Mérindol and watched its devastation from a distance. Their houses were burned down, their harvests ripped from the ground, their wells filled and plugged, and their bridges destroyed. Peasants from the surrounding area followed the soldiers to pillage what was left. The Waldensian men mounted upward and joined their brothers in the villages of La Coste and Cabrières-du-Comtat. In the fortified village of Cabrières, they decided to stand and resist with only three hundred combatants.[10] In the ensuing combat, there were many casualties on both sides. Led by Marron, the Waldensians battled courageously but were no match for the cannons of the enemy. They proposed to open the gates if promised safe passage to Germany or if given a pledge of fair trials. With the promise received, Marron and his partisans exited the village first. They were immediately seized and executed in a nearby meadow. Only Marron and the pastor Guillaume Serre were spared, taken in custody by the pope's legate to Avignon to be judged and burned at the stake. The female combatants were locked up in a barn which was then set ablaze. Those who tried to escape were massacred, their heads carried in triumph on the tips of lances. Soldiers searched for survivors and forced open the door of the church. In the sanctuary women were raped, their throats slit, and some thrown from the bell tower. The few women who survived were sold as slaves at L'Isle-sur-le-Sorgue. In one month, nine hundred houses were burned, twenty-four villages destroyed, and three thousand people massacred. Only the most robust men were spared and sold to spend their remaining days on the king's galley ships. The Parliament made it a crime to assist those in misery dying from hunger. Anyone showing pity suffered the confiscation of their possessions. The cavalry of Agoult, installed at the Tour-d'Aigues, roamed throughout the countryside committing atrocities. Peasants were forced to travel to Aix or Marseille to find and ransom their kidnapped children. When the Parliament sent two members to investigate the barbarism, they returned horrified at the savagery against helpless people. The peasants of Luberon could no longer work their land without soldiers stealing their oxen and women were robbed and assaulted in the fields. Based on this report, the Parliament rendered a new order authorizing the authorities to assist the population.[11]

10. Félice, *Histoire des Protestants* (1), 62–63.

11. Miquel, *Guerres de religion*, 127–33.

The massacre of the Waldensians was met with indignation throughout the kingdom. The king ordered an investigation and demanded an accounting of the expedition. The Cardinal de Tournon supported the cause of Meynier and on August 8, 1545, the king rendered his verdict, approving what was done to exterminate the Waldensians. Calvin and Farel were devastated by the news and requested intervention from the Swiss. The king's justification to the Swiss was that the Waldensians were disloyal subjects and punished because they refused to pay the tithe. At the death of Francis I the tide turned. Meynier sought to continue the persecution and arrested two men with strong connections in Parliament. The cardinal was in a state of disgrace with King Henry II (r. 1547–1559) who designated a commission to investigate the baron and others involved in the crimes. The indictment against Meynier charged him with distorting the truth about the heretics, undertaking the massacres on his initiative, and condemning the vagabonds to die of hunger. His eloquence allowed him to save his head and he expressed no remorse for his actions against the Waldensians. In the end Jean Meynier, Baron d'Oppède, was liberated, restored to his functions, and named chevalier of Saint-Jean-de-Latran by the pope.[12]

CONCLUSION

History has preserved some of the last words pronounced by the Waldensians who took refuge in mountain gorges. Preparing to die, and contemplating from afar the smoking ruins of their homes, they exhorted each other. They said that the least concern they should have was for their earthly possessions and their greatest concern was to remain faithful to their confession of Jesus Christ and his gospel.[13]

What became of the Waldensians? Some escaped to Geneva where they were well received. Others found refuge in

---

12. Miquel, *Guerres de religion*, 134–35.

13. Félice, *Histoire des Protestants* (1), 62.

communities in Dauphiné. In any case, they powerfully aided the Reformed cause in gaining a foothold in the Cévennes and Languedoc regions of France. Several years later, Sébastien Castellion (l. 1515–1563), who ministered alongside Calvin for a time in Geneva, wrote in the preface to his *Traité des hérétiques*, "Who would want to become a Christian when they see that those who confess the name of Christ are bruised at the hands of Christians, by fire, by water, by the sword, and treated more cruelly than robbers and murderers?" [14]

14. Delumeau, *Le christianisme*, 81.

CHAPTER 4

Wars of Religion and Saint Bartholomew's Day Massacre

1562–1598

THE WARS OF RELIGION took place in the second half of the sixteenth century as Protestantism gained ground in France and opposition grew from the monarchy and Catholic Church. By most accounts, there were eight wars or conflicts during this period. The Wars of Religion first broke out in the spring of 1562 and would last for over three decades. Before the wars ended, tens of thousands died and the divide grew between opposing religions.

PROTESTANT GROWTH AND REPRESSION

The decade before the wars broke out was one of the most fruitful periods for the Reformation. Arrests, executions, and confiscations did not fulfill the goals of the persecutors. It became clear that further measures were needed to deal with Protestant heretics. In 1551 the Edict of Châteaubriant attributed to both secular and ecclesiastical judges the authority to address the crime of heresy. Heretics found not guilty by one tribunal could be tried by another for the same crime. One-third of the condemned person's possessions went to the denunciator. The king confiscated the properties of those who fled France and it was illegal to send money or letters to fugitives.[1]

In September 1557, the "Affair of the rue Saint-Jacques" took place. Several hundred Reformed believers gathered to celebrate the Lord's Supper at a house on the street Saint-Jacques behind the Sorbonne. The neighborhood was awakened by theology students at the Sorbonne and residents gathered stones to pelt the believers as they fled the house. Others barricaded themselves in the house. Their lives were spared at the arrival of soldiers only to be attacked as they left the house and taken to prison covered with mud and blood. The executions of several prisoners led to an uproar throughout Europe and the bloodshed ended only when Henry II issued an act of amnesty.[2]

A new phase of violence in the French Reformation was entered when Protestants established public worship. Entire villages and provinces had been won over by the Reformed faith. The sheer number of believers made secret gatherings impossible. Public worship was also seen as the best means of convincing their enemies that lies had been told about them. People could go and see for themselves what was preached and practiced.[3] Beginning in 1560, two years before the wars commenced, lists of Huguenots were created in many cities to deprive people of their rights.[4] One's name on the list meant running the risk of losing all rights each time a conflict broke out. Throughout these times of trouble, cities used these lists to banish Protestants. Constituted in times of peace, often with the complicity of one's neighbors, the lists lay dormant for a few months or a few years until needed in times of war to exile Protestants and claim their properties. The rights of Protestants were ephemeral, their possessions lost overnight, their communities destroyed, and their future compromised. They took up arms to defend themselves, their families, and their religion.

1. Félice, *Histoire des Protestants* (1), 74.

2. Félice, *Histoire des Protestants* (1), 75–76.

3. Félice, *Histoire des Protestants* (1), 103.

4. See Davis, *French Huguenots* (xvi), for a discussion on the origin of the term "Huguenot."

They were often used as pawns for political purposes. They lost all confidence in the stability of a world collapsing around them and in the frayed institutions of their nation.[5]

The eight wars took place interspersed with brief periods of peace, treaties, and compromises. The final war became known as the war of three Henrys between dynastic rivalries—King Henry III, also known as Henry of Valois and earlier as Duke of Anjou; Henry de Lorraine, Duke of Guise (1550–1588); and Henry de Bourbon, Huguenot leader and king of Navarre, the future King Henry IV. During the Wars of Religion, "so frequent and gruesome were the massacres accompanying these conflicts, so searing the sieges, and so numerous the assassinations of leading political actors, that the events of the 'time of religious troubles' burned themselves into French and European historical memory for centuries to come."[6] The civil war in France was also influenced by international events, in particular the revolt and the repression of the subjects of Philip II in Holland which aroused emotions in France. Each side benefited from foreign assistance: the Catholics from King Philip II of Spain (r. 1556–1598), Pope Pius V (p. 1566–1572), and the Duke of Tuscany; the Protestants from William of Nassau, Duke of Orange with whom Louis de Bourbon, prince of Condé (l. 1530—1569) and Admiral Gaspard de Coligny (l. 1519–1572) signed an alliance, and from Queen Elizabeth I of England who financed expeditions in France.[7]

CONFERENCE AT POISSY AND THEODORE BEZA

King Francis II (r. 1559–1560) died December 5, 1560, at seventeen years old after a reign of only eighteen months. His brother Charles IX (r. 1560–1574) became king at the age of ten and their mother Catherine de Medici became queen regent.[8] Catherine understood

---

5. Foa, "Les droits fragiles," 104–05.

6. Benedict, "Wars of Religion," 147.

7. Miquel, *Guerres de religion*, 234.

8. Félice, *Histoire des Protestants* (1), 111–12.

the growing influence and power of Protestantism and sought an accord with the Calvinists. It was one of those moments when the Reformation might have become dominant, humanly speaking, had it not been for the maneuvers of Catherine, the ambition of the house of Guise, the intrigues of the king of Spain, and the opposition of the Catholic clergy. Catherine called a conference on September 9, 1561, at Poissy where Protestant leaders were invited before the king, the royal court, and Catholic prelates. The delegation had ten pastors and twenty-two lay leaders led by Theodore Beza who was sent in Calvin's place. After speeches from the king and chancellor, the delegates of the Reformed churches were introduced as in a courtroom. Beza eloquently expounded Calvinist doctrine and presented the king with a copy of the Reformed Confession of Faith. When Beza explained the Reformed understanding of the Eucharist as the spiritual presence of Jesus Christ he was accused of blasphemy.[9] The Catholic delegation demanded that the Reformed representatives unconditionally accept the authority of the Catholic Church and its teaching of the Eucharist that the elements, bread and wine, are transformed into the body and blood of Christ (transubstantiation). If they refused, they were threatened with anathema and banishment. At this same conference, the Jesuit representative, Jacques Lainez (l. 1512–1565), in a discourse that astonished even many Catholics, compared the heretics to foxes and wolves who did not deserve a hearing. The conference ended on October 9 with one main point highlighted: the hope to unite the two religious confessions through mutual concessions was an illusion.[10]

Despite the outcome of the conference, Reformed believers were strengthened by having the opportunity to expound their faith before the leaders of the kingdom and princes of the Catholic Church. They could no longer be accused of villainous crimes nor be handed over to punishment without due process. Important cities like Milhau, Sainte-Foy, Lacaune, and hundreds of villages broke off from the Catholic Church. Pierre Viret (l. 1511–1571), a

9. Félice, *Histoire des Protestants* (1), 128–31.

10. Félice, *Histoire des Protestants* (1), 133–36.

Swiss Reformed theologian, arrived at Nîmes in October 1561 and spoke before a crowd of eight thousand. During this great religious movement, empty Catholic churches were taken over by Protestants. This led at times to the regrettable destruction of crucifixes, images of saints, and relics. Viret and other Reformed leaders opposed these actions. Many Reformed and Catholic followers could not yet envisage the coexistence of two religious confessions in one place.[11]

The number of Reformed believers reached its numerical peak in 1560 and would steadily decline in the following decades and centuries because of war, plague, exile, and emigration.[12] Historians offer contradictory figures for the number of people in the Reformed confession at this time, from one-tenth to half of the kingdom's population. The cardinal of Sainte-Croix reported the kingdom was half-Huguenot, surely an overestimation. Yet according to Félice, historians who present the number of Reformed believers as only one-tenth of the population fall into the other extreme of underestimation. It is possible that one-fourth of the kingdom was Protestant although this figure would include those who identified with Protestantism for political purposes. One-tenth of the nation, however, would neither have inspired such fear in its adversaries nor would have been capable of defending itself from the other nine-tenths for such a long time during the coming wars of religion.[13] In any case, "the dizzying expansion which Protestantism knew for a brief moment on the eve of the Wars of Religion was halted and reversed by the civil wars and the violence which accompanied them."[14]

11. Félice, *Histoire des Protestants* (1), 137–38.

12. See Benedict, "Huguenot Population of France" for a detailed demographic analysis from 1600 to 1685.

13. Félice, *Histoire des Protestants* (1), 140.

14. Benedict, "Huguenot Population of France," 102–3.

MASSACRE OF PROTESTANTS IN VASSY

On January 17, 1562, Catherine de Medici's Edict of January accorded the Huguenots limited rights for private religious practices in government-approved places. The terms "heresy" and "heretics" were removed from royal legislation and Protestants obtained the freedom of conscience with limited freedom of worship.[15] Large religious gatherings were still forbidden in population centers where the Huguenots were concentrated, Catholic church buildings they had occupied needed to be restituted, and they were forbidden to destroy images or crosses. The Edict of January was rejected by most French Catholics. The authorities of the Church considered Catherine's edict in contradiction to the Council of Trent which had anathematized the heresy of Luther and Calvin. She soon became aware of the dangerous situation in which the edict placed her and sought to placate the Catholic faction. With the Edict of January, Protestants felt they had almost obtained the freedom of worship, but soon they were confronted by violations of the edict. War seemed inevitable.[16]

Francis, Duke of Guise

15. Foa, "Les droits fragiles," 96.
16. Stéphan, L'Épopée huguenote, 103.

The massacre of Protestants in Vassy in the Champagne region in March 1562 signaled the beginning of the Wars of Religion. The power-hungry house of Guise was at the center of intrigues and attempts to rid the kingdom of Huguenots. Francis de Lorraine, Duke of Guise (l. 1519–1563), engaged in subterfuge with German Lutherans and pretended to be favorable toward the Confession of Augsburg in order to separate Lutherans from French Protestants. His mother, Antoinette de Bourbon, shared her son's antipathy toward the Huguenots and was displeased to see the spread of Calvinism in the region.[17] On Sunday, March 1, the duke learned that several hundred Huguenots were meeting in a barn at a time when Reformed worship was forbidden in cities. With two hundred armed men, he came across this large congregation gathered at a short distance from the Catholic Church and attacked them. His soldiers cried "Huguenots, heretics, dogs" as they struck the fleeing worshippers. Some fell to their knees pleading for mercy. None was given. Neither women nor children escaped the slaughter. The pastor, Léonard Morel, was on his knees praying and tried to flee when fired upon. He was trapped by a cadaver at the door, wounded, and led away. None of the executioners dared to kill the pastor and his life was spared.[18]

Accounts of the number of victims vary with estimates of at least sixty killed and two hundred wounded. The incident sparked more massacres and the religious wars were on. After a supposed investigation into the massacre, the story was invented casting the Huguenots as the aggressors. The duke was received in Paris with a triumphal entry and Catholics compared him to Judas Maccabee as the defender of the faith. The Protestant consistory of Paris sought justice and sent Theodore Beza to the royal court. Antoine de Bourbon, the king of Navarre and convert from Protestantism to Catholicism, accused the Huguenots of attacking the duke. Beza replied that the church of God received beatings but did not give them and that this church was an anvil that wore out many hammers. He spoke the truth. Antoine de Bourbon and others like him

17. Stéphan, *L'Épopée huguenote*, 107.
18. Félice, *Histoire des Protestants* (1), 148–49.

fell. The persecutors lie in their tombs and the Protestant Reformation still stands.[19]

Massacre at Vassy

Following the massacre at Vassy, the first war (1562–1563) began as Protestant forces seized cities in which they reportedly destroyed Catholic churches and sacred relics. At Tours, two hundred Huguenots were slain and their bodies tossed into the Loire River. At Sens, Protestants were slaughtered and their bodies were thrown into the Yonne River with the cadavers floating to Paris.[20] Catherine de Medici offered conditions for peace with limitations on Protestant worship, and the Edict of Amboise, also known as the Edict of Pacification, was signed on March 19, 1563. As crippling as it was to the Protestant cause, the edict ended the armed conflict and provided the free exercise of religion in cities that were under the authority of Calvinists. The first war ended, or rather a simple suspension of armed hostilities took place. No one was really satisfied. Catholic fanaticism was rekindled by the

19. Félice, *Histoire des Protestants* (1), 150–53.
20. Stéphan, *L'Épopée huguenote*, 129.

return of the Protestants to a place of favor and in different places attacks against Huguenots continued.[21]

Catherine de Medici

A precarious peace survived for four years following the Edict of Amboise, which suffered multiple violations. During this period Catholic Leagues were formed to oppose concessions to Protestants and for the eradication of heresy. There were legal processes against Protestants who had pillaged Catholic churches. Organized bands attacked the minority Protestants and both sides engaged mercenaries for protection. Certain governors refused to implement the royal decree and threatened the unity of the kingdom. The Huguenots in regions of southern France, in places where they constituted a majority, found the limitations of the Edict of Amboise unbearable and were determined to resist. Violence followed with uprisings in various cities and atrocities were committed on both sides. The Protestants attempted to avenge the humiliation suffered by the Edict of Amboise and took up arms again in 1567.

21. Garrisson, *Histoire des protestants,* 109–10.

This sparked the second war of religion (1567–1568) which ended with the Treaty of Longjumeau in March 1568.[22]

After a brief respite of five months, the third war began in 1568 and advanced with the international participation of Switzerland, Germany, Italy, and England. Religious tolerance came to an end with the decree of Saint-Maur in September 1568. Protestants were forbidden to worship and accused of the crime of treason (*lèse-majesté*). The Edict of Saint-Germain was signed on August 8, 1570, and ended the third war of religion. Protestants obtained a reprieve from their troubles. The edict guaranteed freedom of conscience and freedom of worship in designated locales. The royal power prudently recognized the need to tread carefully with a powerful minority. An appearance of tranquility reigned in France with a semblance of peaceful coexistence. The peace was short-lived, criticized by the Pope, and unacceptable to Catholics with the loss of entire cities no longer under the king's authority.[23]

SAINT BARTHOLOMEW'S DAY MASSACRE

Saint Bartholomew's Day Massacre

22. Stéphan, *L'Épopée huguenote*, 135.

23. Stéphan, *L'Épopée huguenote*, 136–37.

With Reformed believers reestablished in the public life of the kingdom, Catherine de Medici drew closer to Reformed leaders and began to arrange marriages. After having married her son Charles IX to Elisabeth of Austria, she plotted to marry her favorite son Henry of Anjou (l. 1551–1589), later Henry III, to Queen Elizabeth I of England. She arranged a marriage between her daughter Marguerite of Valois (l. 1553–1615) to Henry of Navarre, a Huguenot of the house of Bourbon-Navarre. The marriage of Henry of Navarre to Marguerite took place with great pomp on August 18, 1572. Four days later, on August 22, an attempt was made on the life of Gaspard de Coligny, considered the greatest lay leader of the French Reformation who had taken his first steps toward Reformed teaching in 1555.[24] On returning from the Louvre to his chambers, Coligny was wounded on the arm and hand. The

house where the would-be assassin had hidden belonged to a partisan of the Guise family. A doctor who attended to Coligny's wounds thought the copper balls might have been poisoned. His friends feared for his life. Coligny asked them why they were crying and told them he was happy to have received his wounds in the name of God.[25]

Admiral Gaspard de Coligny

24. Félice, *Histoire des Protestants* (1), 92.

25. Félice, *Histoire des Protestants* (1), 195.

As a result of this failed assassination, tensions rose among the factions and provided the catalyst for the massacres to follow. Municipal leaders were ordered to close the city gates and arm the militia. The Duke of Nevers, Louis Gonzaga, intervened to request that the life of Henry of Navarre be spared.[26] Then the massacre began. Early in the morning of August 24, 1572, a small band of assassins led by the Duke of Guise headed down rue de Béthisy to the inn where Coligny was recovering from his wounds. Soldiers ordered by Charles IX to protect the place where Coligny rested joined the band and attacked the inn, murdered Coligny in cold blood, and threw his lifeless body out a window.[27] A one-day killing spree turned into a season of slaughter. Three days of massacre followed in Paris where two to three thousand Reformed believers lost their lives. As the news from Paris spread to the provinces, the Catholic populations of Meaux, Orléans, Troyes, Bourges, Samur, and Lyon set upon the Protestants to exterminate them. French people carried out the bulk of the carnage against Protestants with thousands of victims. They slit their throats, dragged them through the streets, threw them into rivers, and as if death were not enough of a punishment, mutilated their cadavers.[28]

In certain provinces where Protestants had a greater numerical presence, as in Saintonge and Languedoc, no one dared attack them. Not all Catholics participated in or approved of the slaughter. The bishop of Lisieux, Jean Hennuyer refused to obey the order of a king's envoy to massacre the Protestants. Historians disagree on the number of victims in France with estimates from thirty thousand to one hundred thousand. The last figure is probably exaggerated if only the victims of violent death are counted. But if the number includes those who suffered death from misery, famine, and abandonment, that figure might be less than the actual number.[29] Philip II wrote to Catherine to thank her for the wonderful news. Charles IX and Catherine de Medici were praised by Rome

---

26. Stéphan, *L'Épopée huguenote*, 139.

27. De Waele, "Le cadavre du conspirateur," 97.

28. Garrisson, *Histoire des protestants,* 113–14.

29. Félice, *Histoire des Protestants* (1), 202–5.

for their efforts to annihilate the rebellious heretics. Pope Gregory XIII (p. 1572–1585) had the cannon fired at the Castel Sant'Angelo and a medal was struck in the honor of this great event.[30]

CONCLUSION

As the slaughter continued in the provinces for several months, fearful Protestants defected and reembraced the Catholic religion. A good part of Europe expressed disdain for France and especially for her kings. The massacre relaunched inter-confessional conflict, horrified Protestants and Catholics alike, and remains one of the great crimes of humanity etched into the memory of Protestants.[31] The Saint Bartholomew's Day massacre had not produced its desired effect to rid the kingdom of schismatic Protestants. Over time this reality led to "a growing, if still begrudging, acceptance of the argument that religious toleration was less an evil than endless warfare."[32]

30. Félice, *Histoire des Protestants* (1), 206.

31. Stéphan, *L'Épopée huguenote*, 142.

32. Benedict, "Wars of Religion," 163.

CHAPTER 5

Wars of Religion and the Three Henrys

1562–1598

THE SAINT BARTHOLOMEW'S DAY massacre forced many Protestants to renounce their faith or flee the kingdom and set the stage for the fourth war of religion (1572–1573). Many fled to find refuge abroad or in Protestant-controlled regions in France. Battles raged at Nîmes and Montauban with the cities' refusals to accept royal garrisons. La Rochelle was besieged by royal troops under the command of the Duke of Anjou, the future Henry III. After failing to take the city, the Edict of Boulogne was signed in July 1573. The edict granted freedom of worship in the cities of La Rochelle, Montauban, and Nîmes, and the freedom of conscience to all Huguenots.[1]

HENRY III

Henry III (r. 1574–1589) was the third son of Henry II and Catherine de Medici. During the reign of his brother Charles IX, he had two victories at Jarnac and Moncontour in 1569 over the Huguenots. He had been elected king of Poland in 1572 and returned to France at the death of his brother in 1574. His reign was

---

1. Stéphan, *L'Épopée huguenote*, 143–44.

53

inaugurated with authoritarian measures and he was pressured by his mother Catherine to wage war against the Huguenots. Protestants in the south of France organized a confederation of provinces. They had lost their confidence in the king and gained assurance in their capacity to resist oppression.[2] Catherine found intolerable the questioning of royal authority in the provinces and any consideration of a Protestant state. For her, the kingdom was not a subject of discussion or negotiation.[3] These events led to the fifth war of religion (1574–1576).

Duke of Anjou (Henry III)

2. Stéphan, *L'Épopée huguenote*, 148.

3. Miquel, *Guerres de religion*, 302–3.

War and Politics

The fifth war lost some of its religious character as a political conflict against tyranny. Henry III's brother, Francis, Duke of Alençon (l. 1555–1584) left the royal court in September 1575, found refuge in his fief at Dreux, and allied himself with Henry of Navarre. In October 1575, the Duke of Guise, attempting to save the monarchy, won a battle against the avant-garde of the army marching toward Paris. The victory was spectacular but not decisive. Catherine sought to make peace with her son Francis and yielded to his demands to save her own crown. Under her influence, a treaty was signed at Champigny which guaranteed a truce among the royals until June 1576. Protestants were granted the freedom of worship in all the cities where they were masters, and several other cities were turned over to Protestant control. An edict of pacification, known as the Edict of Beaulieu, was signed on May 6, 1576. The king took great care to express his regrets for the events of the Saint Bartholomew's Day massacre. Under the edict's terms, Reformed worship was allowed throughout the kingdom except for Paris and immediate surrounding areas. Protestants were permitted access to all employments and all court proceedings against the Protestants were suspended, seized possessions were restituted, and Protestants were permitted their own cemeteries. Yet Protestants were still obliged to pay the tithe to the Catholic clergy. The Catholic religion was reestablished everywhere and Catholic churches were established in towns under Protestant control.[4]

By all measures, the Edict of Beaulieu was by far the most liberal of all the edicts promulgated since the beginning of the Wars of Religion and met most of the demands made earlier by Protestant leaders. Henry of Navarre became governor of Guyenne, received authorization from the king to return to his holdings, and was reimbursed for the debts incurred by his mother at the time of his marriage.[5] Protestant victories exasperated Catholics and embittered the king. Catholics were furious when they learned of the

4. Miquel, *Guerres de religion*, 314–15.
5. Miquel, *Guerres de religion*, 315–16.

concessions made to the Protestants under the edict. The king's legitimacy was questioned for allowing Reformed believers to freely worship and for surrendering cities to Protestant control. Opposition came from Catholics who formed defensive coalitions.[6]

Broken Treaties

In a short time, the Edict of Beaulieu was revoked and armed conflict resumed, commencing the sixth war of religion. Protestants lost several cities including La Rochelle and negotiations led to the Treaty of Bergerac in September 1577. This treaty was later confirmed by the Edict of Poitiers, signed the following month in October 1577, and followed the main points of the Edict of Beaulieu with new restrictions. Protestants were no longer in a position of strength to negotiate more favorable terms. Reformed worship was limited in many places. The zone of exclusion around Paris was enlarged and the Huguenots were guaranteed several more years of security for eight strongholds.[7] The continued presence of the Catholic League after the Edict of Poitiers presented more disadvantages than advantages for Henry III. The king feared the Duke of Guise who used the League to further his own schemes, forming a political party, finding resources, and gathering men for his cause. The queen mother warned her son of the dangers and the king realized the error he made in becoming the head of the League. Dissolving the League might have ended the Wars of Religion had it not been for princely rivalries. In the quest to advance their own interests, a seventh war loomed on the horizon.[8]

The Edict of Poitiers was not widely received and in many places was not executed. There were divisions among the royal family and anarchy throughout the kingdom. Catherine de Medici met with Henry of Navarre and leaders from churches in Languedoc. The negotiations resulted in the Treaty of Nérac on February

---

6. Miquel, *Guerres de religion*, 321–22.

7. Stéphan, *L'Épopée huguenote*, 149–51.

8. Miquel, *Guerres de religion*, 326–28.

28, 1579, to provide clarification for the terms of peace. Catherine consented to respect the security of Protestant strongholds for six months, but she refused to grant freedom of worship. She settled for short-lived treaties to satisfy her vanity and give her the role of mediator.[9] The seventh war (1579–1580) which followed the Treaty of Nérac was on a smaller scale than previous ones and became known as the war of princes. Several skirmishes took place before the signing of the Treaty of Fleix in November 1580, which merely confirmed the Edict of Poitiers. Protestants were promised six years to retain their strongholds without royal interference. To many people, the seventh war seemed unnecessary and largely motivated by personal interests and rivalries.[10]

Final War

This eighth war of religion (1585–1598) is often presented as the war of the three Henrys—Henry III, Henry of Guise, and Henry of Navarre, with the latter Henry eventually victorious. With the death in 1584 of Francis of Alençon, the last brother of King Henry III, Henry of Navarre became a legitimate heir to the throne.[11] The prospect of a Protestant king led to the formation of another Catholic League led by Henry of Guise. Cardinal Charles de Bourbon (l. 1523–1590), the uncle of Henry of Navarre, was declared the sole candidate for kingly successor under the name of Charles X. Henry of Guise, dreamed of the crown for himself and fancied himself a descendant of Charlemagne.[12] This announcement triggered the eighth war of religion which saw little action until the Battle of Coutras on October 20, 1587. The Protestant army led by Henry of Navarre with five to six thousand poorly equipped men faced off against ten to twelve thousand well-armed Catholics commanded by Anne, Duke of Joyeuse (l. 1561–1587). At the

9. Stéphan, *L'Épopée huguenote*, 151.

10. Stéphan, *L'Épopée huguenote*, 152.

11. Miquel, *Guerres de religion*, 330.

12. Stéphan, *L'Épopée huguenote*, 153.

moment of battle the Protestants fell to their knees and sang Psalm 118:24, "This is the day that the Lord has made; let us rejoice and be glad in it." The enemy interpreted this as a sign of weakness, attacked, and was soundly defeated. Anne of Joyeuse and half his army died on the battlefield. Navarre won a great victory, ordered care for the wounded, set the prisoners free, and testified of his sorrow for this great spilling of French blood.[13]

Assassinations

In October 1588, Henry III solemnly swore an oath to abolish heresy. At the same time, the king warned the members of the Catholic League that they endangered Catholicism through their factiousness. After he overhauled his government, the king decided to destroy the League which he considered dangerous for the monarchy and peace. Henry III dreamed of eliminating his archenemy the Duke of Guise who flattered himself by boasting that he held the king prisoner. The king resolved to follow the counsel of his entourage who advised the king that it was not possible to rid himself of his antagonist by normal means of justice. Two months later, on December 23 at the Château de Blois, Henry of Guise was summoned by the king and stabbed to death by the king's guards.[14] News of his death spread rapidly. Paris took up arms and the Sorbonne proclaimed the king deposed. Outward signs of the monarchy were destroyed and images of the king were lacerated. For many, Henry III was no longer the king of France and was declared a tyrant. The Sorbonne freed the people from their oath of fidelity to the Crown. Parliament members who had remained faithful to the king were treated disrespectfully and the most ardent royalists were arrested. The League named the Duke of Mayenne as lieutenant general of the armies to replace the assassinated Henry of Guise.[15] Henry III took shelter in Tours where the Parliament was

13. Félice, *Histoire des Protestants* (1), 232.

14. Félice, *Histoire des Protestants* (1), 233.

15. Stéphan, *L'Épopée huguenote*, 158–59.

transferred. The Duke of Mayenne headed to Tours with his horsemen and scattered the royal forces at Amboise. Henry III, chased from Paris, had no other choice than to seek reconciliation with Henry of Navarre for a common front against the duke. They met on April 30, 1589, at the Château de Plessis-lès-Tours, an ancient manor of Louis XI (r. 1461–1483). At his arrival, Navarre kneeled before Henry III who embraced him. With an army of over forty thousand men commanded by the two kings, they marched to the gates of Paris.[16]

In Paris, the population railed against their sovereign for forming an alliance with the Protestant heretics. Jacques Clément, a Dominican monk belonging to the Catholic League, decided to take action in August 1589. He obtained a meeting with Henry III at Saint-Cloud and requested permission to deliver a private message to the king. Alone with the king, Clément stabbed Henry III in the stomach as he leaned in to better hear the message. The assassin was immediately killed by the king's guards. That evening, shortly before his death, joined by Henry of Navarre and attended by physicians, the king enjoined Henry of Navarre to convert to Catholicism and recognized him as his successor.[17]

Henry III succumbed to his wounds after eighteen hours and the house of Valois ended. Of his predecessors, Francis I died in diseased agony; Henry II was mortally wounded in a jousting tournament; Francis II died at a young age; Charles IX died in the convulsions of an unknown illness; Francis, Duke of Alençon, died in debauchery; and Henry III died at the hands of an assassin. The house of Valois, with the blood of martyrs on its hands, and which had sought to exterminate the Protestant religion, had come to its deserved end.[18]

16. Félice, *Histoire des Protestants* (1), 236–37.

17. Miquel, *Guerres de religion*, 353–54.

18. Félice, *Histoire des Protestants* (1), 237.

HENRY OF NAVARRE'S COMPROMISE

Henry of Navarre had become the heir presumptive to the throne of France when Francis, Duke of Alençon died in 1584. Now with the death of Henry III, he became king as the head of the house of Bourbon and would struggle for several years to secure his kingdom. France needed a king capable of opposing Philip II of Spain. Catholics knew that Navarre disapproved of the murder of the Duke of Guise. They also recognized him as a valiant prince from his exploits in battle. Moderate Catholics held in common with Navarre the hatred of the pope, fear of the Spanish, and disdain for the Guises. They were ready to welcome a king who could reestablish peace and guarantee the coexistence of two religions. Yet to be king, Navarre needed to be chosen not simply crowned. There was opposition from the Catholic League and many nobles who refused to recognize him as Henry III's successor. Once again the king was invited to convert and refused.[19]

On August 4, 1589, Henry of Navarre promised that the Catholic religion would maintain its place of preeminence and that he would seek instruction in this religion within six months. During this time, Catholics and Protestants would keep their respective places and Reformed worship was limited to the places where it was already observed. Based on this promise, many rallied to his cause and desired a return to order and the cessation of violence.[20] During the years 1588 and 1589 Henry of Navarre multiplied military activity in Normandy and around Paris. His royal troops, composed of Protestants and Catholics, defeated the Duke of Mayenne at Arques near Dieppe in September 1589 and besieged a resistant Paris. During this period, Charles X, king of the League and prisoner of the royals, died. Navarre continued to battle in Normandy, failed to take Rouen and Orléans, and suffered several defeats. Navarre demanded recognition as king before his conversion. Catholic priests in Paris swore to die before accepting Navarre as king, even if he converted. In the end, Navarre

19. Miquel, *Guerres de religion*, 355–59.
20. Miquel, *Guerres de religion*, 361.

understood that as a Huguenot he would never be accepted by the Catholics. For hostilities to cease, Navarre confirmed his intention to convert to the Catholic religion.[21]

CONCLUSION

For over thirty years during the Wars of Religion, Protestants survived in times of prohibition and temporary legality. The loss of rights they had obtained did more to shatter the Protestant momentum than the absence of rights.[22] It is estimated that from 1570 to 1598 Protestants lost 30 percent of their places of worship. They found themselves on the outside of a Catholic and royal consensus. For half a century Reformed believers were hunted, massacred, exiled from their cities, chased from their offices and places of employment, deprived of basic rights, and wearied by financial sacrifice.[23] There were further struggles as Henry IV worked to rid the kingdom of Spain's influence. The clemency of the king toward those who had viciously resisted him won over much of the opposition. The crowning moment of Henry IV's reign would arrive with the Edict of Nantes in 1598.

21. Miquel, *Guerres de religion*, 383–86.
22. Foa, "Les droits fragiles," 107.
23. Garrisson, *Histoire des protestants*, 67–70.

CHAPTER 6

Henry IV and the Edict of Nantes

1598

HENRY OF NAVARRE BECAME the nominal ruler of France after the assassination of Henry III of France in 1589, whose marriage to Louise de Lorraine produced no heir. After years of attempts to deny the throne to Navarre, his enemies realized they could not defeat him militarily. The French Wars of Religion had exhausted the country, and as we saw in the previous chapter, Henry would need to adopt the religion of the majority of his subjects to assure the freedom of conscience for Protestants with whom he had a religious affinity and who had fought by his side.

The arrival of a Protestant king and the weariness of opposing parties imposed the compromise of Henry's conversion to Catholicism. The Archbishop of Bourges announced Henry's intention on May 17, 1593, and on July 25 Henry of Navarre solemnly recanted in the Basilica of Saint-Denis at the feet of the archbishop.[1] His abjuration was attacked as feigned by some, a political decision, yet many citizens simply wanted peace and a nation free from foreign influence. The archbishop was considered a traitor by some radical Catholic factions. They claimed that the pope alone had the authority to reconcile an excommunicant to the Church. There were attempts on Henry IV's life by Jean Barrière in 1593 and Jean

1. Stéphan, *L'Épopée huguenote*, 168–69.

Châtal in 1594. Many cities accepted Henry's conversion with conditions that included banning Protestants from gathering in the cities and surrounding areas of Paris, Rouen, Meaux, Poitiers, Agen, Beauvais, Amiens, Saint-Malo, and many other places.[2] Protestants did not hide their chagrin and requested guarantees from the king who promised to reestablish an earlier edict of 1577 and its guarantee of religious tolerance. Protestants were permitted to worship throughout the kingdom, even discreetly at the court, and army officials could celebrate the Lord's Supper in the camps. With these conditions, the Protestants provisionally maintained their confidence in their former co-religionist.[3]

Henry IV of France

2. Félice, *Histoire des Protestants* (1), 251.

3. Miquel, *Guerres de religion*, 388.

Religious and political leaders eventually rallied to Henry, which led to his coronation as King Henry IV of France at the Cathedral of Chartres on February 27, 1594. There he pronounced the traditional oath to drive out from his lands all heretics denounced by the Church. On March 22 the king entered Paris and the *Te Deum* rang out from Notre Dame.[4] Pope Clement VIII (p. 1592–1605), vexed by the French Church's absolution of Henry IV without pontifical authorization, distrusted the sincerity of the king. Not until September 1595 did the pope confer his conditional pardon. Protestants, however, ulcerated by the king's abjuration, feared that reconciliation with the pope would lead to renewed persecution and sought to obtain further guarantees of security.[5]

EDICT OF NANTES AND RELIGIOUS TOLERANCE

In response to continuing religious violence, on April 13, 1598, the king promulgated an edict of pacification and declared it perpetual and irrevocable: the Edict of Nantes. The edict imposed religious coexistence and was met with resistance. Henry IV deployed his energy to obtain the registration of the edict in regional parliaments. Rome continued to oppose any change in the Catholic Church's privileged position in France, and Pope Clement VIII declared that freedom of conscience was the worst thing to have ever happened. After years of religious wars, the edict did not immediately extinguish all the grudges and resentment, but it opened a new period in relations between Catholics and Protestants and provided relative security and tolerance for Protestants. The Peace of Vervins, signed on May 5, 1598, between Henry IV and Philip II of Spain, brought a temporary entente between the two nations and contributed to Henry IV's rising stature in the affirmation of his power and the stability of his reign. The birth of Louis XIII assured the perennity of the dynasty.[6]

4. *Te Deum* is Latin, short for *Te Deum laudamus* (God we praise You), and was sung on occasions of public rejoicing.

5. Stéphan, *L'Épopée huguenote*, 172–73.

6. Giraudier, "La rébellion du duc de Bouillon," 339.

The Edict of Nantes was a watershed in French history and Henry IV's crowning achievement. France established the concept of tolerance and officially proclaimed that people were free to profess the religion of their choice, although Catholicism would remain the religion of the kingdom. This was an edict of compromise previously unknown in France, granting legal recognition of the Protestant religion and setting limits to Protestant worship.[7] Protestants were still required to pay tithes to Catholic parish priests, observe Catholic feast days, and all religious property that had originally belonged to the Catholic Church was ordered returned. In some places, in and around Paris and other cities, Protestant worship was forbidden within an established radius. Protestants and Catholics had equal rights in providing education for their children. From a political point of view, full amnesty was granted for all acts of war. Civil equality with Catholics was guaranteed, and there was a provision for the right of access to public employment. Those who had fled France were allowed to return.[8]

The edict opened access for Protestants to universities and public offices, and four academies were granted authorization along with the right to convoke religious synods. Protestants were guaranteed the security of their garrisons for eight years in several towns, most notably the port city of La Rochelle. One great innovation was that civil power placed limits on religious domination of society. The Catholic Church recuperated two hundred cities and two thousand rural parishes and resigned itself to tolerance as a necessity of the present circumstances. While Protestants were not allowed missionary activity to open new places of worship, Catholics altered the religious map, opening churches in places where Catholicism had virtually disappeared.[9]

7. Daireaux, "Louis XIV et les protestants normands," 124.
8. Stéphan, *L'Épopée huguenote*, 173.
9. Miquel, *Guerres de religion*, 407.

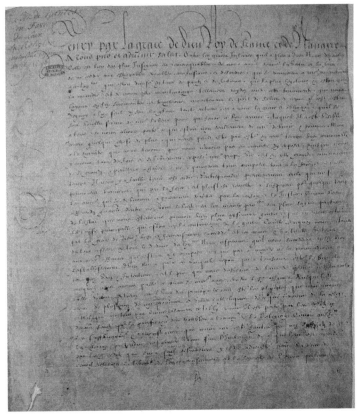

Edict of Nantes

In reality, the Edict of Nantes was a treaty of pacification with concessions designed to prevent further warfare. The edict, in granting tolerance toward Protestants, also reinforced the rights of the Catholic Church. Article three stipulated that the Catholic, Apostolic, and Roman religion would be reestablished throughout the kingdom to be freely and peacefully exercised without any trouble or obstacle. This authorized the complete institutional restoration of the Catholic Church in every corner of the kingdom, even in places where the majority of habitants had converted to the Reformed faith, in cities like La Rochelle, Montauban, and Montpellier, and in vast regions like the Cévennes, Dauphiné, and

Vivarais. In all these places, Protestants now needed to prepare for the return of priests who had been absent for two generations.[10] Catholic processions resumed in places where there had been none for decades. Tensions were often high in cities with two places of worship, two cemeteries, two categories of the king's subjects, and even two church bells.[11] Protestants retained territorial possession of strongholds in more than one hundred cities in France, including La Rochelle, Saumur, Montpellier, and Montauban. During this period of tolerance, these cities became semi-autonomous states within the kingdom. They held political assemblies, developed territorial organizations, maintained military fortresses, and practiced diplomacy and relations with foreign powers, notably England. La Rochelle became the principal bastion of the Reformed religion and was supported by England, which sought to curb the development and expansion of the French navy.[12]

The first ten years of the seventeenth century following the Edict of Nantes marked a Catholic renewal. The king flattered himself that France might return to religious unity. To this end, funds were established (*caisse de conversion*) to pay pastors who converted to Catholicism. The times changed from religious wars to religious controversies and were marked by conversions between the two religions; monks embraced the Reformed religion, and pastors turned toward Catholicism. Henry IV had several Protestant collaborators, and to his credit during his reign, he lifted his war-torn nation out of decades of civil war. However, he refused to reunite the Estates-General and create a parliamentary monarchy that might have protected the nation from coming abuses of power. He oriented the nation toward absolutism which offered him a stunning if brief splendor which would lead to bloody reactions.[13]

10. Birnstiel, "La conversion des protestants," 95–96.
11. Miquel, *Guerres de religion*, 409.
12. Lacava and Guicharnaud, *L'Édit de Nantes*, 3.
13. Stéphan, *L'Épopée huguenote*, 204–5.

LOUIS XIII AND PROTESTANT STRONGHOLDS

The edict was enforced during the reign of Henry IV, at times with great difficulty, until his assassination on May 14, 1610. He had survived multiple plots and attempts to assassinate him before falling at the hand of a Catholic zealot, François Ravaillac. His death alarmed the Protestant community that feared the loss of its acquired rights. Following her husband's death Marie de Medici (l. 1575–1642), the second wife of Henry IV, became queen regent from 1610 to 1617 during the minority of her son Louis XIII. She confirmed the Edict of Nantes in a declaration on May 22, 1610, but Protestants had little confidence in her. The Estates-General gathered in 1614 and 1615, at which the Protestants perceived that the nobility and the clergy were prepared to consider the edicts of pacification as provisory. They were also alarmed by the proposed marriage of Louis XIII to Anne of Austria (l. 1601–1666). Three provinces, Languedoc, Guyenne, and Poitou took part in an uprising led by malcontent lords. Marie's negotiations with them resulted in the Treaty of Loudun in 1616, which granted six more years of protection for Protestant strongholds.[14]

Long before its revocation in 1685 under Louis XIV (r. 1643–1715), the edict and its protections were undermined through inconsistent application and interminable bad faith complaints lodged against Protestants. The Edict of Nantes had not established equality between the religions. Protestants received political advantages and were simply tolerated as long as they practiced their religion within the strictures imposed on them. The presence of Protestant strongholds, however, became intolerable for Henry IV's successor, his son Louis XIII (r. 1610–1643). Under him, the domination of the Catholic clergy grew rapidly. The king took a Jesuit for his confessor, and his new minister, Charles-Albert de Luynes, pledged to exterminate the heretics. At the general assembly of Catholic clergy in 1617, Louis XIII, instead of respecting the will of his father, ordered the restitution of possessions to the Catholic Church. He marched on to the province of Béarn, took

14. Stéphan, *L'Épopée huguenote*, 206–8.

the stronghold of Navarriens, and reestablished Catholicism. The abuses committed against a majority Calvinist population foreshadowed the future *dragonnades*, a form of persecution under Louis XIV where Protestants were forced to lodge the king's cavalrymen (*dragons*) to induce Protestants to convert to Catholicism.[15]

Louis XIII of France

In response to the king's actions, the Huguenot general assembly at La Rochelle in December 1620 divided France into eight quasi-military regions with leaders, which triggered Catholic opposition. Many Protestants in southern France took up arms, but the rest of the country did not move against the king. Louis XIII

15. Félice, *Histoire des Protestants* (1), 279–80.

went on to besiege Montauban, which resisted heroically for two and a half months and forced the king to lift the siege on November 2, 1621. The king besieged Montpellier in August 1622, but the city defended itself so valiantly that the king agreed to negotiate. The siege was lifted and the Peace of Montpellier was signed on October 18, 1622, confirming the Edict of Nantes and granting amnesty, but forbidding political assemblies without royal authorization. Only two stronghold cities remained: La Rochelle and Montauban. The years 1622 to 1625 were marked by incessant squabbles and acts of violence. In 1625, Henry de Rohan (l. 1579–1638) in Languedoc and his brother Soubise in the western regions engaged in military campaigns without decisive results.[16]

CARDINAL RICHELIEU
AND THE SIEGE OF LA ROCHELLE

Marie de Medici had succeeded in introducing Armand du Plessis de Richelieu (l. 1585–1642) into the court of Louis XIII in 1624. Richelieu was the prime minister during the reign of Louis XIII. He was a man of great ambition and capacities, a strict defender of the Catholic cause in France, and intended to break all opposition to royal absolutism. Louis XIII and Richelieu sought to force the submission of Protestants to royal authority and reinforce the unity of the kingdom. The city of La Rochelle stood as a formidable barrier to their designs and had become the principal stronghold of the Huguenot party.[17] Richelieu did not hide his intention to establish the absolute authority of the king on the ruins of La Rochelle. Louis XIII announced this intention to the pope who had been troubled by reports of a treaty with the Huguenots. The archbishop of Lyon wrote to Richelieu to encourage the siege of La Rochelle, to punish, or even better, to exterminate the Huguenots.[18]

---

16. Garrisson, *Histoire des protestants*, 127.

17. Delumeau, *Le christianisme*, 97.

18. Félice, *Histoire des Protestants* (1), 295.

La Rochelle had largely adhered to the Protestant Reformation, was responsible for the dissemination of Protestantism in western regions of France, and had become a refuge for Protestants fleeing other places. The city had been besieged several times during the Wars of Religion without success. Coligny, Jeanne d'Albret, and Henry of Navarre had found refuge behind her walls. Political assemblies were held there during difficult times. La Rochelle was the most secure and well-armed city of the French Reformation.[19] Richelieu's attempts to negotiate with La Rochelle failed in 1625, and he was forced to sign the Treaty of Paris in February 1626. In 1627 the conflict was reignited and La Rochelle was besieged for a year, encircled, and cut off from all outside provision. Richelieu ordered the construction of an enormous dike to prevent all help from the sea. The last months of the siege were marked by a devastating famine, obliging women, children, and the elderly to leave the city and wander destitute through the marshes, where few survived. Those besieged survived by eating horses, dogs, and cats, with hundreds dying daily of famine. La Rochelle had a population of twenty-five thousand before the siege, of which eighteen thousand were Protestant, and little more than five thousand inhabitants when the blockade ended.[20]

19. Félice, *Histoire des Protestants* (1), 296.
20. Stéphan, *L'Épopée huguenote*, 211–13.

Richelieu on the Sea Wall of La Rochelle

The expedition mounted by the Duke of Buckingham failed due to his assassination and La Rochelle capitulated on October 28, 1628. The next day Richelieu entered the city and celebrated a solemn Mass in the Church of Sainte-Marguerite. Louis XIII entered La Rochelle on November 1 to receive its surrender, followed by a great procession on November 3. The king abolished all the former benefits the city enjoyed, ordered most of the ramparts leveled, turned the temples[21] over to the Catholic Church, and created a bishopric. After years of sacrifice, La Rochelle's destiny was now tied to the French monarchy and the Catholic Church.[22] There was a great celebration at the news of La Rochelle's capitulation in Rome. A *Te Deum* was raised to heaven and Pope Urban VIII (p.

---

21. French Protestant church buildings were referred to as temples which distinguished them from Catholic edifices that were called churches.

22. Stéphan, *L'Épopée huguenote*, 214–15.

1623–1644) made an extraordinary distribution of indulgences. He assured the king that God was at his right hand.[23]

The slaughter continued when the royal army marched on the little city of Privas in May 1629. The inhabitants, seized with panic, fled to the countryside. There was an explosion as the king's troops entered the city. They believed it was an ambush and slaughtered eight hundred Huguenot soldiers. Richelieu then ordered the destruction of all fortifications in Huguenot cities.[24] In June 1629, with the Edict of Grace (Peace of Alès), negotiated by Richelieu with Protestant leaders, Protestants experienced the loss of many earlier gains. The edict maintained the concessions of the Edict of Nantes but dismantled the Protestant party. Reformed pastors had the right to preach, celebrate the Lord's Supper, baptize, and officiate at marriages only in villages and cities authorized by the Edict of Nantes.[25]

CONCLUSION

Protestants were now considered factious in the face of a centralized unity sought by the great ministers, Richelieu and later Mazarin. Protestants lost their princes and protectors. Henry de Rohan was the last armed leader of the French Reformation. What his sword did not accomplish would be fulfilled in God's time. He offered his services to the Republic of Venice and met his death on the plains of Germany for the same cause he had defended valiantly for so long in his own country.[26] Louis XIII ordered the demolition of Protestant strongholds and the re-establishment of Catholic worship. Although Protestants theoretically retained religious rights for another fifty years, they lost political influence and were progressively excluded from public functions.[27] In 1665

23. Félice, *Histoire des Protestants* (1), 301.

24. Félice, *Histoire des Protestants* (1), 302.

25. Miquel, *Guerres de religion*, 401–2.

26. Félice, *Histoire des Protestants* (1), 304–5.

27. Stéphan, *L'Épopée huguenote*, 216–17.

clergy accompanied by a magistrate were authorized to present themselves at the house of terminally ill people to ask if they wanted to die in heresy or convert to the true religion. That same year children were declared competent to embrace Catholicism, boys at the age of fourteen, and girls at the age of twelve. The Catholic Church argued in vain to lower the age of consent to whenever a child expressed a desire to convert or in many cases was induced to convert.[28] The rights of Protestants were contested, their family life undermined, and eventually completely lost in 1685 with the Revocation of the Edict of Nantes to which we now turn.

28. Félice, *Histoire des Protestants* (1), 344–45.

CHAPTER 7

Louis XIV and the Revocation of the Edict of Nantes

1685

AS WE HAVE SEEN, beginning in the sixteenth century Protestants in France struggled in their rapport with royal power. Protestants owed the recognition of their rights more to sovereign decrees than to genuine tolerance or religious pluralism. The realization that the monarch held the authority to revoke what had been granted led to suspicion and mistrust toward rulers. Under Louis XIV (r. 1643–1715) and the Revocation of the Edict of Nantes, they lost the rights gained under Henry IV. This was not the first time that a sovereign required his subjects to adopt his religion. Generally, however, subjects were given a choice between conversion or emigration. Louis XIV refused to allow Protestants to leave the kingdom, except for pastors who were ordered to leave, and deprived Protestants of public worship, pastors, legitimate marriages, and temples. They lost freedom of worship and freedom of conscience.[1]

---

1. Encrevé, *Les protestants*, §318–42.

EDICT OF NANTES UNDERMINED

Louis XIV of France

Louis XIV, known also as the Sun King (*le Roi Soleil*), was one of the most illustrious French kings. His reign was marked by cultural and military achievements as well as endless wars and religious intolerance. During the reign of his grandfather Henry IV, the effects of the Edict of Nantes in 1598 allowed French Catholics and Protestants to cohabitate in an uneasy peace. After the death of Henry IV in 1610, the Catholic Church and monarchy plotted the removal of protections provided under the Edict of Nantes. Beginning in 1630 the Catholic clergy sought to counter heresy through traveling monks and other hirelings who disputed with Protestants. Some even attended Reformed gatherings only to afterward argue with attendees outside the meeting place and contest the preacher's sermon. These attempts at conversion obtained little success. What could not be accomplished by attempts to convert Protestants through words led eventually to forced conversions by the sword.[2]

Cardinal Mazarin

Early in Louis XIV's reign, there was a season of religious tranquility for Protestants. With Cardinal Mazarin (l. 1601–1661) at his side, Louis XIV initially thought that strict respect for previous edicts and the refusal to grant additional rights was the most effective way to reduce the number of Protestants in his kingdom. Mazarin himself exercised tolerance in granting employment and government positions to Protestants, and he did not give satisfaction to the complaints of Catholic clergy who protested the construction of Protestant temples. A royal declaration in 1652 recognized Protestant fidelity to the Crown and promised the maintenance of the Edict of Nantes with the enjoyment of all its

2. Félice, *Histoire des Protestants* (1), 313–15.

benefits. In 1656 this declaration was revoked and the exercise of Reformed religion was forbidden in places where it had recently been established. Provincial synods sent a delegation to present their grievances to the king who authorized them to hold a general synod in November 1659 at Loudun. The king's representative reproached the members of so-called Reformed religion (*religion prétendue réformée*) in attendance for their insolence and supposed violations of edicts, and announced that this would be their last national synod. The royalty had already broken the Huguenot political party and now, influenced by the Catholic Church, crushed the religious community.[3]

The death of Mazarin in 1661 was a loss for Reformed believers. He had not inspired confidence and was not their friend but preferred to use cunning rather than force. Louis XIV was now determined to become the absolute master of his kingdom. In 1679 the Peace of Nimègue with the European powers was the pinnacle of his renown. He received the title of "Grand," was praised by the courtesans, and was treated as a demigod. The entire kingdom was considered his property and he was the supreme judge and the only legislator.[4] With hostile measures, he sought to paralyze Protestant vitality and bring about conversions to Catholicism. The king established the Commissions as the principal means of repression through which he sent commissioners into the provinces to investigate reported or supposed violations of the Edict of Nantes.[5] Reformed churches were placed in an accusatory posture and had to justify their existence while Catholic Church representatives argued systematically for the closure of Reformed churches, schools, and charitable works. Dozens of churches were forcibly closed in the provinces of Bas-Languedoc and the Cévennes where there were about 140,000 Protestants, or religionnaires as they were called.[6] The Catholic clergy obtained a declaration in 1663 against the "relapsed," that is, those who returned to the Reformed

---

3. Félice, *Histoire des Protestants* (1), 322–23.

4. Félice, *Histoire des Protestants* (1), 360–61.

5. Félice, *Histoire des Protestants* (1), 342.

6. Bost, *Prédicants Protestants*, 6–7.

community after having converted to Catholicism. They were no longer protected by the Edict of Nantes since they returned to heresy and were liable to criminal charges of desecration of holy mysteries and subject to banishment. Many historians consider this the first major attack on the Edict of Nantes and the first step toward its revocation.[7]

EDICT OF NANTES REVOKED

Revocation of the Edict of Nantes

7. Félice, *Histoire des Protestants* (1), 343–44.

The conflict became more bitter beginning in 1679, and the legal insecurity of the 1660s and 1670s was replaced by measures to dismantle Protestant churches and intensify repression. Catholic conversion to Protestantism was banned, and Protestant converts to Catholicism were forbidden to return to their former religion. In 1681 a royal edict declared that the children of Reformed believers could convert to Catholicism at the age of seven. Families were shaken and lived in fear and distrust of friends and neighbors. A priest, an enemy, or a disgruntled debtor needed only to declare before a judge that a child had made the sign of the cross, kissed an image of the Virgin, or wanted to enter a Catholic church. This was often enough to remove the children from their parents' home, especially the homes of the rich, who were forced to pay for lodging at a convent under the direction of monks or nuns.[8]

Louis XIV no longer sought to undermine the Edict of Nantes but was now determined to bypass it. The king unleashed the ferocious *dragonnades* which constrained Protestants to lodge the king's troops to accelerate conversions. Apart from being forbidden to kill the inhabitants, the soldiers were authorized to do all in their power to obtain conversions. They committed horrible crimes of passion, savagery, and theft. Neither women, the elderly, nor children were spared from the atrocities committed by royal troops. Women were whipped, struck with rods to disfigure them, and dragged by the hair through mud and stones. Multitudes fled to the forests, hid in the houses of friends, or sought refuge across the borders.[9] Reformed believers in Vivarais and Dauphiné took up arms in desperation. Although promised amnesty, fifty prisoners were sent to the king's galleys. The pastor Isaac Homel, seventy-two years old, was accused of fomenting the uprising, condemned to the rack, and received thirty lashes before the executioner finished him off on October 16, 1683.[10] The Huguenots were ready to offer the king their possessions and their lives but not their consciences. In a matter of only a few years, the Protestant situation

8. Félice, *Histoire des Protestants* (1), 364–65.

9. Félice, *Histoire des Protestants* (1), 368–69.

10. Félice, *Histoire des Protestants* (1), 374.

in France radically and perilously reversed. The Reformation had been solidly rooted in many provinces by the middle of the seventeenth century. Reformed churches had benefitted from favorable conditions created by the Edict of Nantes. Churches and synods had been well organized, led by quality leaders, and demonstrated loyalty toward royal power. Now the most prominent temples were demolished and the number of Protestant adherents dwindled.[11]

The prohibitions were multiplied: Protestants were forbidden to congregate outside their authorized places of worship and permitted to worship only at specific times; they were forbidden to sing the Psalms during worship; pastors were forbidden to stay in one place for more than three years; marriages between Catholics and Protestants were forbidden; ceremonies of baptism or marriages were limited to twelve persons; burials were forbidden during the day and only ten persons allowed to gather; pastors were forbidden to criticize the Catholic Church in any way, and they were forbidden to receive new converts into churches under threat of banishment and confiscation of property. Those hospitalized were pressured to convert and visited by magistrates to obtain a renouncement of Protestantism. Most Protestant schools were closed and parents were not allowed to send their sons abroad for studies. Little by little, Protestants lost virtually all the rights granted by the Edict of Nantes.[12]

Catholic clergy persuaded the king that the success of these measures had diminished the Reformed religion through conversion or emigration to the point where few Protestants were left in France. When he discovered otherwise, the clergy lay the blame on the obstinacy of the Protestants and the inability of priests to combat heresy. Louis XIV finally yielded to the clergy's pressure to obtain the Revocation of the Edict of Nantes on October 18, 1685, also known as the Edict of Fontainebleau. The king's subjects were compelled to adopt the religion of the king. By this edict, Louis

11. Daireaux, "Louis XIV et les protestants normands," 129.

12. Stéphan, *L'Épopée huguenote*, 226–29.

XIV "destroyed the Protestant Church in France, but he had not destroyed Protestantism."[13]

Articles of Revocation

The articles of the Edict of Revocation reveal the drastic measures undertaken to remove the last vestiges of the Protestant religion from France. The preamble contained the lie that the majority of the king's subjects of the so-called Reformed religion had embraced the Catholic religion and the Edict of Nantes was no longer needed.[14] Article one ordered the demolition of Protestant temples. Articles two and three forbade all religious assemblies with the threat of prison. Articles four, five, and six ordered the expulsion within fifteen days of all Protestant pastors who refused to convert to Catholicism and the inducement of lifetime pensions for those who converted. Article seven outlawed Protestant schools. Article eight obliged all infants to be baptized into the Catholic Church and receive religious instruction from village priests. Articles nine and ten ordered the confiscation of possessions of those who already emigrated unless they returned within a specified period. Protestant emigration was forbidden under the threat of galleys for the men and imprisonment for the women. Article eleven stipulated punishment for new converts who refused the sacraments of the Church. Article twelve granted the right to remain in the kingdom to not-yet-enlightened Protestants conditioned by the prohibition of assemblies for worship or prayer. The Catholic Church opened centers of conversion and Protestantism no longer had the right to exist in the kingdom.[15]

---

13. Poland, *Protestantism in France*, 27.

14. Félice, *Histoire des Protestants* (1), 383.

15. Carbonnier-Burkard, *La révolte des Camisards*, 17–19.

Conversion and Confiscation

The fear of the *dragons* led to waves of conversions among entire villages and accelerated the disappearance of Protestants. In only a few months, hundreds of thousands of Protestants converted to Catholicism and were placed under strict surveillance. Of course, there is the question of whether forced conversions were sincere conversions. And many Catholics regarded these "new converts with suspicion and scorn and thereby forced them to reconsider their conversions."[16] The Revocation reestablished the union of the Church and monarchy and provided material benefits for the royal family. Over six hundred Protestant temples were ransacked and destroyed, and the Jesuits suggested that the plunder be given to the king. The possessions of individuals were targeted as well for distribution among the king's loyalists, religious and otherwise. With the population decimated by periodic famines and dying of hunger, Louis XIV left the royal palace at the Louvre in Paris and settled at Versailles in 1682 surrounded by his court. Versailles became his principal residence and was expanded and embellished at exorbitant cost, the ostentatious symbol of his power and influence in Europe. There he and his courtesans reveled in sumptuous living off the proceeds of confiscated possessions. Counted among the beneficiaries were abbots and bishops of the Catholic Church, shamelessly profiting from the plundering of Protestants, now fugitives and exiles.[17] The death penalty was pronounced in July 1686 against pastors who returned from exile, the king's galleys the fate of those who lent them assistance, and the death penalty for anyone caught in an illegal assembly.[18]

Exile

The number of exiles is difficult to determine. Hundreds of thousands of Protestants escaped and emigrated to places of refuge

16. Poland, *Protestantism in France*, 28.
17. Janzé, *Les Huguenots*, §623.
18. Félice, *Histoire des Protestants* (1), 400.

including Geneva, England, Germany, and Holland. Among them were soldiers, sailors, magistrates, intellectuals, merchants, and craftsmen whose departure impoverished France and enriched her neighbors. Of the approximately 780 pastors still in France in 1685, 620 went into exile and 160 abjured, although some later returned to the Reformed faith.[19] Entire villages were abandoned and cities half-deserted. Voltaire estimated that fifty thousand families left the kingdom over a period of three years; Antoine Court spoke of eight hundred thousand persons; a writer hostile to the Reformation after consulting genealogical lists estimated 225,000, perhaps a more realistic figure.[20] Forty percent of Protestants in the northern provinces of the kingdom crossed the borders of France to find safety, while only 16 percent in southern regions including Languedoc and Provence, and 2 percent in the Cévennes region fled the country. The majority of those who remained, two-thirds of Reformed believers, did not convert to Catholicism and began to organize themselves, first in small groups and later in large assemblies in out-of-the-way places. Less than a month after the Revocation, the Edict of Potsdam under Frederick William, Elector of Brandenburg and Duke of Prussia, encouraged Protestant refugees to relocate to Brandenburg and granted them the same rights and privileges as those born there. The losses to France following the Revocation went beyond the loss of money and people. As fragile and complicated as the peace had been since 1598, the societal benefits of stability were real in creating schools and businesses. When Louis XIV began to shrink the Protestant space, those gains were sacrificed and France lost any hope of peaceful coexistence.

The Revocation of the Edict of Nantes offered a façade of unity. Through state violence, France falsely believed she had rediscovered national and spiritual unity. Historians rightly observe a connection between the religious terror of 1685 and the revolutionary terror of 1793. In 1685 Louis XIV treated the cursed Protestants as outlaws. One hundred years later the French monarchy and the French clergy paid dearly for their tyranny. The victors

19. Carbonnier-Burkard, *La révolte des Camisards,* 20–23.

20. Félice, *Histoire des Protestants* (1), 394.

of the Revocation became the victims of the Revolution. Louis XVI and his family were massacred by their subjects. Priests were forced into exile and found refuge among the descendants of those whom their predecessors had persecuted.[21]

CONCLUSION

Paul Deschanel (l. 1855–1922), deputy of Eure-et-Loir and later president of the French Republic, called the Revocation of the Edict of Nantes one of the greatest crimes ever committed against the human conscience.[22] The religious persecution of Protestants following the Revocation has made them the representatives of the great cause of freedom of conscience. Their repeated requests for justice and their oaths of allegiance to the Crown all failed at the foot of the throne of despots. Only in 1787 with the Edict of Toleration would French Protestants be considered fully French with the right to marry before a civil official, register the birth of their children, and bury their dead. Full recognition for Protestants as truly and legally French would come only with the much-maligned French Revolution in 1789, and Protestant legal equality with Catholicism was finally achieved under the Napoleonic Concordat and Organic Articles in 1801 and 1802 which will be discussed in chapter eleven. Before those better days arrived, another war was on the horizon.

21. Cabanel, "Enchanter, désenchanter l'histoire," 414–15.
22. Bruley, La séparation, 279.

CHAPTER 8

War of the Camisards in the Cévennes

1702–1705

THE WAR OF THE CAMISARDS WAS launched by Protestant Huguenots in the Cévennes region of southern France. After the Revocation of the Edict of Nantes in 1685 by Louis XIV, Huguenots
worshipped and married illegally in secret places before rising up
to reclaim their religious rights. This last armed struggle of the
French Reformation cannot be compared with any past wars.
During the last war of religion in the sixteenth century, Henry of
Navarre had entire provinces and half the French nobility behind
him. Now we find poor peasants who knew little about the art of
war, armed only with farming instruments and weapons taken
from their enemies, and sacrificing their lives behind the bushes
and rocks of their mountains. They had no nobles to lead them
nor the bourgeoisie of the plains and cities to support them. These
were people considered insignificant who sacrificed their lives for
the cause of religious freedom.[1]

RETURN FROM EXILE

After the Reformed religion was outlawed by the Revocation of
the Edict of Nantes, Protestant temples were destroyed and pastors

1. Félice, *Histoire des Protestants* (1), 413.

were exiled. The Huguenots saw themselves as metaphoric Hebrews and their leaders adopted names associated with the Jewish people of the Old Testament—Josué Janavel, Abraham Mazel, Salomon Couderic, and Élie Marion, among others. Huguenots in the Cévennes worshipped and wandered in the woods of this region. The preachers of the Cévennes were often considered seditious rebels working hand in hand with France's enemies to deliver the province to foreign powers. Exiled pastors returned to the Cévennes in 1689 at great risk to their lives. These men were united in their desire to reestablish Protestant worship and were bound by the conviction that state-authorized and state-coerced religion was not in conformity with biblical teachings. Among them was Claude Brousson (l. 1647–1698), perhaps the most famous clandestine preacher, who had self-exiled to Geneva and Lausanne and returned to France to preach and organize secret nighttime gatherings. He entitled his collection of sermons, "The Mystical Manna of the Desert."[2] Another returnee was François Vivent (l. 1664–1692) who had refused to renounce his faith in 1685 and had been hunted down before being authorized to leave France in 1687.

Although Vivent, Brousson, and their companions returned to France to awaken the zeal of new converts, they also intended to join the coalition of William of Orange (l. 1650–1702) in the hope of confronting Louis XIV with a formidable insurrection. They received promises of support from England, Switzerland, and Holland. As attested in letters written by Pierre Jurieu (l. 1637–1713) and Brousson, the persecuted church sought above all the freedom to practice their religion—freedom offered to them under Henry IV and snatched away by Louis XIV. Both Brousson and Vivent became martyrs; Vivent was killed in a cave defending himself on February 19, 1692, and Brousson was executed at Montpellier on November 4, 1698.[3]

---

2. Janzé, *Les Huguenots*, §623.

3. Stéphan, *L'Épopée huguenote*, 265.

Prophetic Epidemic

On their return to France, Brousson and Vivent also addressed what has been called a "prophetic epidemic" which was rampant in regions deserted by pastors.[4] In the absence of pastors, prophets and prophetesses proliferated in Dauphiné, in Vivarais, and especially in the Cévennes. In the beginning, these self-appointed leaders preached the gospel, exhorted repentance, and promised freedom. In time, claiming inspiration from the Spirit and nourished by the Old Testament, many fell into mystical trances and preached revolt. Most Protestant pastors disapproved of their activities and attributed the excesses to the lack of spiritual guides. Early prophetic manifestations were peaceful until 1702. As arrests and executions increased, the prophetic message changed into a call to holy war and armed resistance.[5]

CAMISARDS

The origin of the word "Camisard" as a description for Cévenol insurgents is disputed. According to some, they owe their name to the white shirt they wore over their clothing in order to be recognized among themselves.[6] Others see a reference to an old word "*camisade*" (night attack) or "*camin*" in patois referring to paths along mountain ridges.[7] Over 50 percent of the Camisard warriors were younger than twenty-five years old, mostly from rural or semi-rural regions. Over two-thirds were artisans in textile; one-third were shepherds or farmers. The wives and sisters of the Camisards followed the troops and at times also wielded the sword. The Protestant nobility was largely absent, while some became active in the repression of their co-religionaries.[8] The Camisards called themselves the "children of God," "people of

---

4. Krumenacker, *Marie Durand*, 79.

5. Miquel, *Guerres de religion*, 209–10.

6. *Nouveau Petit Robert*, 335.

7. Stéphan, *L'Épopée huguenote*, 266.

8. Carbonnier-Burkard, *La révolte des Camisards*, 55–56.

God," "flock of God," and addressed their leaders as "brothers." They carried out reprisals against their persecutors, both priests and soldiers. They punished their own who committed murder or acts of depredation. They held all things in common, had caverns for hospitals, and often dressed in the garments of defeated enemies. Their numbers at any one time rarely exceeded a thousand men, with approximately ten thousand men engaged in guerilla warfare throughout this period. When victors they held religious assemblies. When vanquished they found refuge in impenetrable gorges.[9]

Jean Cavalier

The war had its beginning in July 1702 when the prophet Pierre Séguier, called Esprit Séguier, declared during an assembly that the Spirit had called him to liberate prisoners arrested and tortured by the abbot of Chaila at Pont-de-Montvert. Accompanied by Abraham Mazel, Séguier and forty men marched

9. Félice, *Histoire des Protestants* (1), 416–17.

all night and surrounded the presbytery. They forced open the doors, freed the prisoners, killed the abbot, and set the edifice on fire. Emboldened by their success, they set fire to two churches and killed eleven Catholics. Three of the attackers were captured and tortured, Séguier among them, who was burned at the stake at Pont-de-Montvert. The Camisards wreaked havoc throughout the Cévennes under the leadership of Abraham Mazel, Gédéon Laporte, Jean Cavalier, and Salomon Couderc. They practiced the Old Testament law of the talion, destroying churches in response to their temples being burned down, and putting fear in village priests who sought refuge in cities.

François de Langlade, Abbot of Chaila

During their first military encounter in September 1702, Laporte and Cavalier faced off against soldiers led by Captain Poul. A month later, Laporte and several of his men were surprised in a ravine and killed, their heads exposed on the bridge of Anduze as a warning to the insurgents. Laporte's nephew Pierre Laporte (l.

1680–1704), later known as Rolland, and Cavalier, sheep castrator and shepherd respectively, led small groups of poorly armed peasants for two years in guerrilla warfare against the king's troops. The success of the Camisards was partly due to their knowledge of the rugged countryside with its woods, ravines, mountains, and caves. They had the complicity of newly-converted Catholics and were feared by other Catholics. They held frequent worship gatherings and sang "Let God arise" from Psalm 68 before attacking the enemy with fury. The royal troops often fled at the intonation of the first notes of the Camisard hymn.[10]

In December 1702, the Camisards addressed a letter with their demands to Victor-Maurice, Count de Broglie (l. 1647–1727), commander of the royal forces. They wrote that they simply wanted the freedoms purchased with the blood of their ancestors and that they were prepared to die rather than renounce their beliefs. Because the edicts of the king had deprived them of their right of public assembly to worship, they had withdrawn into the mountains and caves. They expressed their confidence that the God of mercy had poured out his Spirit on them according to the promise of the prophet Joel and they were constrained to now offer their bodies and possessions in sacrifice for the holy gospel and spill their blood for this just cause. The following month, the Count pursued two of Cavalier's lieutenants, Abdias Maurel, nicknamed Catinat, and Ravenel, with three companies of mounted troops near Nîmes. The Count was defeated and Captain Poul was killed in battle.[11]

TRUCE AND BETRAYAL

Skirmishes and punitive expeditions dragged on in the early months of 1703. In March, the united troops of Rolland and Cavalier were soundly defeated at Pompignan. New converts to Catholicism from Mialet and Saumane, suspected of aiding and abetting the Camisards, were deported to Perpignan. On Palm

10. Stéphan, *L'Épopée huguenote*, 267–69.
11. Carbonnier-Burkard, *La révolte des Camisards*, 60–61.

Sunday, April 1, about three hundred Protestants assembled for worship at a mill near Nîmes. When field marshal de Montrevel was informed about it, he led a troop of soldiers with orders to break down the door and slit the throats of all present. Irritated by the time-consuming process of the slaughter, he burned down the mill. All perished except for one young woman saved from the flames by the humanity of one soldier. The young woman was hanged the next day and her liberator spared at the last minute through the intercession of nuns.[12] There were further attempts to depopulate the Hautes-Cévennes through the methodic destruction of villages, followed by reprisals from Rolland against Catholic villages and Camisard victories led by Cavalier. A promise of amnesty was made in June 1703 for those who laid down their arms and was interpreted by the Camisards as a sign of weakness. Cévenols whose homes had been destroyed swelled the ranks of the Camisards. The combats continued with both resounding victories and stinging defeats for the insurgents.[13]

Cavalier and de Villars

12. Félice, *Histoire des Protestants* (1), 419.

13. Carbonnier-Burkard, *La révolte des Camisards,* 70.

The court at Versailles was greatly concerned about the war and learned that Holland and England were in contact with the insurgents and had promised them support. The court feared an intervention by a fleet of ships and the prospect of fifty thousand combatants on the kingdom's soil. Finally, Louis XIV sent field marshal de Villars to Languedoc as a replacement for Montrevel with assurances of limited freedoms. This new proposal led to defections among the Camisards, and Cavalier himself proposed negotiations. A meeting took place between de Villars and Cavalier at the garden of Récollets outside Nîmes.[14] Cavalier was seduced by de Villars' offer to form a regiment of Camisards of which he would be colonel, and he also accepted a verbal promise of freedom of conscience. The king had no intention of having a regiment of Camisards among his troops, and Cavalier and one hundred of his men were escorted by the king's soldiers from the province with promises unfulfilled, never to return.[15]

The remaining Camisards considered Cavalier a traitor and banded together with Rolland, who refused to surrender and awaited assistance from his allies. He was betrayed by a young cousin and delivered to Nicolas de Lamoignon de Bâville (l. 1648–1724), who governed Languedoc from 1695 to 1718. Trapped in the Château of Castelnau-Valence, Rolland was shot to death on August 14, 1704, while attempting to flee; his cadaver was dragged through the streets of Nîmes, and his five companions were executed. After Rolland's death, the Camisards were demoralized. One by one their leaders surrendered and were allowed to leave the kingdom for Switzerland.[16]

CONCLUSION

There was one final attempt at revolt in the spring of 1705, but the conspiracy was discovered and the perpetrators were severely punished. Several of Cavalier's and Rolland's men were seized and

14. Félice, *Histoire des Protestants* (1), 420–21.

15. Armogathe and Joutard, "Bâville et la guerre des camisards," 44.

16. Miquel, *Guerres de religion*, 507–11.

executed at Nîmes. Among them, Henri Castanet (l. 1674–1705), leader of the Mont Aigoual region, was captured and died on the rack before ten thousand spectators at Montpellier. Catinat and Ravenal were captured and executed at Nîmes, dressed in shirts covered with sulfur and burned at the stake. Only Abraham Mazel remained, who after his escape from prison attempted an insurrection in Vivarais. He and sixty peasants resisted for one year against the royal troops before his betrayal and death on October 7, 1710. His companions were hanged or put to death on the rack.[17] Although the decades to come brought persecution, imprisonment, and exile, Protestants continued their struggle for freedom of worship and paid a price for their conviction. This war had a double effect– Protestants were reassured of their capacity to resist, and meeting stiff resistance, the royal court was apprehensive about its strategy of oppression. During the rest of the eighteenth century, the Huguenots' adversaries feared them and hesitated to push them to their limits.[18]

17. Stéphan, *L'Épopée huguenote*, 270–73.
18. Félice, *Histoire des Protestants* (1), 422.

CHAPTER 9

Huguenot Heroes

Antoine Court (1715) and Marie Durand (1730–1768)

WE HAVE SEEN THAT Louis XIV largely based the Revocation of the Edict of Nantes on the fiction that the vast majority of Protestants had converted to Catholicism. The Protestant religion was outlawed and authorities made attendance at the Mass and catechism mandatory. For the stubborn and non-compliant, there were different means of pressure—fines, lodging troops in homes, the king's galleys for men, and prison for women caught at unauthorized gatherings. France had prisons scattered throughout the kingdom. In the north, the châteaux of Guise and Ham; in the west, at Saint-Malo, Saumur, Angers, Niort, and Angoulême; in the south, at Carcassonne, Ferrières, and Aigues-Mortes. When more space was needed, dissidents were transported to the Antilles from Languedoc. The regions of southeast France—Vivarais, Cévennes, Dauphiné, and Bas-Languedoc—provided the majority of victims. Protestants were deported, imprisoned, or executed, and over two hundred thousand emigrated from France to places of refuge. Of those who remained, thousands were persecuted and charged with treason for practicing their faith.[1]

1. Carbonnier-Burkard, *La révolte des Camisards*, 95.

Several years after the War of the Camisards and the execution of Abraham Mazel in 1710, Louis XIV issued a declaration in March 1715 stating that all subjects of the king were also subjects of the Catholic Church. The falsehood persisted that there were no longer any Reformed believers in France. Anyone who declared that he or she wanted to live and die in the so-called Reformed religion, whether they recanted or not, was considered Catholic and the refusal of the sacraments exposed them to punishment. They were not allowed to leave France. And since they remained in France and the practice of their religion was abolished, they were Catholics.[2]

Toward the end of Louis XIV's reign, the hostility of the Catholic Church to new converts and the shame of those who made insincere conversions "combined to produce the materials with which the French Protestant Church could be rebuilt."[3] In defiance of the king's decree, Antoine Court (l. 1696–1760) gathered a small group of believers to lay new foundations for Reformed churches in France. Protestant believers continued to meet clandestinely and were arrested and condemned for worshipping illegally in the decades to follow. Among those imprisoned was Marie Durand (l. 1715–1776), who stands apart in French Protestant history for her courage in the struggle for freedom of conscience. She was held prisoner for thirty-eight years in the Tower of Constance at Aigues-Mortes in the south of France, liberated in 1768, and returned to her natal village. Many have had their stories told; most have remained nameless in the shadows. Here are the stories of Antoine Court and Marie Durand.

2. Félice, *Histoire des Protestants* (1), 424–25.

3. Poland, *Protestantism in France*, 31.

Assembly in the Desert

CHURCH OF THE DESERT

Following the Revocation of the Edict of Nantes, an estimated three-fourths of Protestants renounced their faith. Those who remained in the south of France worshipped illegally, some in homes, others in secret places. This period became known as the Church of the Desert. By 1700, most pastors were either dead or in exile. In the absence of pastors, self-appointed prophets and prophetesses multiplied and called for armed resistance. In defense of their homes and religious liberty, peasant warriors launched the War of the Camisards to reclaim their lost religious rights.[4] They were emboldened by early victories, yet in the end, they were no match for heavily armed royal forces. One by one their leaders surrendered or were killed. Survivors were allowed to leave the kingdom for countries of refuge.

---

4. Chamson, *Suite Camisarde*, iii.

In abandoning violence, the Church of the Desert entered a new phase in 1715 under the leadership of Antoine Court. The years 1715 to 1760 became known as the "heroic period" of the Church of the Desert when Protestant gatherings were forbidden and those arrested were severely punished. The assemblies took place during the day when the danger subsided, and at night when the risks increased. Time and place were announced only a few hours before the meeting by trusted messengers. Unarmed sentinels stood guard on high places to signal the approach of soldiers. Rarely did a pastor spend more than a few days in one place. Wandering from place to place, often disguised and at times using fictitious names, they hid as if they were lawbreakers. Worship in the wilderness had the same simplicity as in times of freedom: liturgical prayers, singing Psalms, preaching, and the Lord's Supper. There was always the sentiment of danger as they stood and worshipped in the presence of their sovereign Lord.[5]

Antoine Court's Early Years

From humble beginnings, Antoine Court became known for remarkable exploits of faith during a long and sorrowful period in French history. Court was born in Villeneuve-de-Berg in Vivarais and was baptized in the Catholic faith as required by law. He accompanied his mother to the illegal assemblies of the Church of the Desert where prophetesses had replaced exiled pastors. Following the non-realization of prophecies, he broke with the movement of prophetism, rejected violence previously associated with the Camisards, and fought to reverse the consequences of the Revocation of the Edict of Nantes. Court considered four conditions necessary for the reorganization of Reformed churches: regular public gatherings, the disavowal of the disorder caused by those claiming the Holy Spirit's inspiration, the establishment of church order through consistories and synods, and rigorous training for pastors.

---

5. Félice, *Histoire des Protestants* (1), 431–32.

The execution of this plan was accompanied by great difficulties.[6] Yet on August 21, 1715, only ten days before the death of Louis XIV, the most powerful monarch of Europe, Court organized the first synod of the Church of the Desert at Montèze to replant the church which Louis XIV had sought to abolish.[7]

Louis XIV's death sparked great hope among the Huguenots, both in the kingdom and in exile, for the re-establishment of the Edict of Nantes. Their hope did not long survive. Of the six signatories of church regulations adopted at the synod, four were executed.[8] After the arrest of a young preacher, Étienne Arnaud, Court opposed a project to forcibly liberate Arnaud who was put to death by hanging at Alès in the presence of a large crowd on January 22, 1718. His death had a great impact on Protestants beyond the Cévennes region; he was honored as a martyr for the cause of freedom. Two years later, in the region of Nîmes, another assembly was called with Court and other leaders of the Church of the Desert. The king's troops intervened, and Court escaped, but fifty others were arrested. As an example to others, twenty men were initially condemned to the king's galleys for life before the sentence was commuted to deportation. They were transported through France to La Rochelle and exiled to England.[9]

6. Félice, *Histoire des Protestants* (1), 429.

7. Stéphan, *L'Épopée huguenote*, 275.

8. Félice, *Histoire des Protestants* (1), 430.

9. Joutard, "Antoine Court," 75–76.

Louis XV

Louis XV

Louis XV (r. 1715–1774), known also as Louis the Beloved, reaffirmed the Edict of Revocation with the Declaration of 1724 proclaiming France a Catholic nation. Protestants who had converted to Catholicism and then returned to Protestantism were considered "relapsed" and were subject to harsh penalties. The declaration contained eighteen articles. They included condemnation for life to the galleys for men and imprisonment for life for women, with confiscation of possessions for participation at non-Catholic religious gatherings. Pastors again faced the death penalty. Parents were ordered to have their infants baptized by the parish priest and children were required to follow Catholic catechism until the age of fourteen. There was no legitimate marriage apart from its celebration in the Catholic Church. Certificates of catholicity were required for employment and higher education. In all of history, there have been few occasions when a government has so monstrously violated the natural, human, civil, family, and religious rights to this degree.[10]

Although the royal decree was applied sporadically and inconsistently throughout the kingdom, there was great consternation among Protestants. Submission was unthinkable, further emigration might announce the end of French Protestantism, and armed revolt would annul the decision ten years earlier when Protestants had chosen a strategy of non-violence. Their response had two parts. On one hand, they planned to organize peaceful public gatherings to demonstrate to the authorities that French Protestants still existed in the kingdom. The assemblies would disperse at the announcement of the arrival of troops. On the other hand, they would refuse to participate in Catholic ceremonies, particularly baptism, marriage, and extreme unction. It fell to Antoine Court at a synod in 1725 to convince Protestants of the wisdom of these actions. He reminded his listeners of Louis XIV's attempt to destroy Protestantism and how through the years God had raised up leaders to sustain his people.[11]

Antoine Court's Writings

In his writings, Court addressed what he believed was the greatest problem in reorganizing Reformed churches—the War of the Camisards. He emphasized a distinction between the present assemblies of the Church of the Desert organized by pastors and past assemblies characterized by prophecies and violence. Although never a Camisard himself, he admitted that at the age of eighteen he came under the influence of prophetesses. At that time he wrote

10. Félice, *Histoire des Protestants* (1), 433–35.

11. Garrisson, *Histoire des protestants*, 199.

letters to priests in which he threatened a new uprising if persecution continued. In his rejection of self-proclaimed prophets
and prophetesses, his goal was the return of churches to the pre-
Revocation pastoral model of leadership, to refrain from violence,
and to submit to political authority. This change of strategy had
the intention of winning the battle of public opinion in France
and among those in exile. Although he separated from those who
claimed prophetic inspiration, he remained surrounded by many
who had participated in the War of the Camisards. For those who
had experienced systematic persecution, conversion to non-violent
resistance was difficult to accept. In his book, *Histoire des troubles
des Cévennes*, Court showed how intolerance and the dearth of
spiritual leadership contributed to the impossibility of controlling
processes that led to violence instigated by the prophetic utter-
ances of Camisard leaders. He insisted that the situation following
the rebellion influenced his strategy of non-violence, which was
more consistent with evangelical principles. Yet to his opponents,
Court remained a prisoner of a mindset that accorded undeserved
reverence to the monarchy.[12]

In 1729, Court left France permanently to find refuge at Lausanne. There he founded a seminary in 1730 which he directed until his death in 1760. Through his writings, he continued defending
Protestants from accusations of treason against the monarchy.[13] In
his later writings, he sought to reconcile the early Camisard period of violence with the non-violent reorganized Church of the
Desert under his leadership. It seems, however, that he could not
admit that the insurrection of the Camisards facilitated the passage to non-violence and that the fear of a new uprising held the
authorities in check. His collection of over one hundred volumes
of testimonies and letters from galley slaves and exiles constitutes
the greatest and most varied source of the history of the Church
of the Desert.[14]

12. Joutard, "Antoine Court," 76.

13. Bost, *Histoire des Protestants*, 168.

14. Joutard, "Antoine Court," 77–78.

Marie Durand

MARIE DURAND'S EARLY LIFE
AND IMPRISONMENT

Marie Durand was born in 1715 in the hamlet of Bouchet-du-Pranles, in the Vivarais region of southern France, the daughter of Étienne and Claudine Gamonet. The Durands were a deeply religious Protestant couple, forcefully converted to Catholicism following the Revocation of the Edict of Nantes. Their children were compelled to attend Mass and catechism and received Protestant instruction in secret. Marie's older brother Pierre assisted Antoine Court and the Church of the Desert and was later consecrated to the ministry. On January 29, 1719, Étienne was arrested by the king's soldiers during a secret worship service in his home at which Pierre was preaching. Pierre escaped to Switzerland, his mother Claudine was imprisoned at the citadel of Montpellier, and their home was destroyed. Pierre later returned to France to preach and married Anne Rouvier, the sister of a friend who had been condemned to the king's galleys. The authorities again arrested Pierre's father in 1729 and imprisoned him for fourteen years.[15] When her brother fled into exile and her father was imprisoned, Marie found herself alone. Her solitude might explain her marriage at the age of fifteen in April 1730. Against the advice of her brother Pierre, she married Mathieu Serre in secret, a man twenty-five years her senior. Their time together was brief. Only a few months after their secret marriage both Marie and Mathieu were arrested. Mathieu was taken to Fort Brescou and released twenty years later in 1750. Marie was imprisoned in the Tower of Constance at Aigues-Mortes in the south of France. Upon her arrival, Marie joined twenty-eight other women, mostly prophetesses from Languedoc and Vivarais. Imprisoned for being the sister of a pastor, she spent thirty-eight years there in inhumane conditions. Apart from children born there, she was the youngest prisoner. Two years into her imprisonment, her brother Pierre was arrested and executed by hanging. Despite her great sorrow, she rose to lead the imprisoned women and wrote letters for herself and others to request help or to stay in contact with their families. These letters, of which about fifty have been found, have contributed to her renown in providing detailed information about life in the Tower of Constance. In her tower prison, there is an inscription that can be seen today engraved in stone—"Resister." Although there is no evidence that Marie wrote this, that single word captures the courage of women who suffered rather than deny their faith.[16]

15. Krumenacker, *Marie Durand*, 80.

16. Krumenacker, *Marie Durand*, 81; Kirschleger, "Mon âme est en liberté," 569.

Tower of Constance

Life in the Tower of Constance

The Tower of Constance in the medieval town of Aigues-Mortes in the Languedoc-Roussillon region of southern France dates to the thirteenth century. The thirty-three-meter high tower was erected along with a château under Louis IX (r. 1226–1270). The origin of the name is contested but some believe the tower was named after Constance, daughter of Louis VI (r. 1108–1137). Aigues-Mortes was an insignificant, isolated port town surrounded by swamps. In 1574, the town came under Huguenot control, and in 1576, it was declared one of eight safe havens for Protestants under the terms of the Edict of Beaulieu. The Edict of Nantes in 1598 preserved this special status. A Huguenot garrison was quartered there until its fall in 1622 after a siege led by Cardinal Richelieu during the reign of Louis XIII. After the Revocation of the Edict of Nantes in 1685, the Tower of Constance was transformed into a royal prison for religious dissenters. Beginning in 1715, the tower was reserved for women found guilty of attending illegal gatherings of the Church of the Desert. The women and their children born in the tower lived in wretched conditions of extremes of heat in summer and cold in winter. They occupied two vaulted rooms between walls several meters thick. During their years of imprisonment, they were supported with gifts from their friends in Switzerland and France. Their captivity served as an example to frighten others who might dare to disobey the royal edict forbidding Protestant gatherings.[17]

From time to time, prisoners were freed upon conversion to Catholicism; some died in the tower, and others arrived to fill their ranks. Among the four new prisoners who arrived in 1737 was Isabeau Menet, a friend of Marie convicted of attending an illegal gathering with her husband, François Fialès. He was sentenced to the king's galleys and died in 1742. Isabeau suffered from a mental breakdown and was released to her family in 1749. Seven more women arrived from the Cévennes in 1742. In 1761, the last prisoner, Jeanne Darbon of Beaucaire, entered the tower and was liberated on order of the king a month later.[18] Apart from those who recanted their faith or received a special dispensation, the first women were set free in 1762 thanks to a new military commander, and only eleven prisoners remained in 1766. Prince Charles of Beauvau (l. 1720–1793) obtained the liberation of the remaining prisoners. Marie was freed on April 14, 1768, and the last three detainees, Suzanne Bouzigues, Suzanne Pagès, and Marie Roue were freed in January 1769. Marie returned to her natal village, Bouschet-de-Pranles where she lived with Marie Vey-Goutète, a companion in captivity. She died in July 1776, aged and infirm beyond her years.[19]

17. Bost, *Histoire des Protestants*, 181–82.

18. Garrisson, *Histoire des protestants*, 215.

19. Krumenacker, *Marie Durand*, 82.

CONCLUSION

Antoine Court found himself confronted by questions that go beyond his time and resonate in the twenty-first century. When is armed resistance justified in the face of tyranny and state-sanctioned violence? How do we differentiate between legality and legitimacy? What sustains people in times of persecution? Even if Court did not always have the right response, he asked the right questions. Although he adopted a strategy of non-violence and submission to political authority, his objective remained the same as the Camisards'—obtain the freedom of conscience, the freedom to be born, to live, and to die outside a state religion. His writings and position on relations between religion and state and the fear of a new Camisard uprising undoubtedly contributed to the religious tolerance that eventually gained ground in Languedoc and throughout France.[20]

Thanks to the world of art Marie Durand has a visage, immortalized more than a century after her death by the painter Max Leenhardt. In the 1892 painting, Marie stands among weary women on the upper terrasse of the tower. Her finger points heavenward in a posture of unshakeable submission to the divine will. Her letters provide information on conditions in the tower and about her correspondence with Protestants in exile. Yet little is known about Marie's daily life in confinement or her spiritual struggles during thirty-eight years of imprisonment.[21]

---

20. Carbonnier-Burkard, *La révolte des Camisards*, 96.
21. Kirschleger, "Mon âme est en liberté," 570.

Huguenot Women Prisoners at the Tower of Constance

In the history of French Protestantism, Antoine Court and Marie Durand personify peaceful resistance against religious oppression. They did not live to see Protestants granted tolerance in 1787 or religious freedom in 1789. They have been largely forgotten by the French public and remain virtually unknown outside of France. Their memory, however, lives on as an example to those in the struggle for freedom of religion and conscience.

CHAPTER 10

French Revolution

1789–1799

THE FRENCH REVOLUTION WAS more than an event. It was a series of events that played out for a tumultuous decade. Up until 1789, there may not have been any other Christian population that was persecuted longer than Reformed believers in France. Now the sword of intolerance would turn against the persecutors during the worst days of the Revolution. The period introduced a constitutional monarchy, the disestablishment of the Catholic Church, a brief Reign of Terror (*La Terreur*) in 1793 and 1794, the executions of King Louis XVI (r. 1754–1792) and Marie Antoinette (l. 1755–1793), and the inauguration of a new political order. The arrival of the Revolution broke with the model of governance of the *Ancien Régime* with its societal divisions and the mingling of church and state in the affairs of the citizenry.[1] The absolute monarchy legitimatized by divine right was replaced theoretically by the sovereignty of the people. In reality, sovereignty was often exercised by government bodies with dictatorial powers who trampled the rights of the people.[2]

---

1. *Ancien Régime* describes France's political and social system under a monarch prior to the Revolution in 1789.

2. Maira, "Luther révolutionnaire," 101–2.

Protestantism won ground throughout the kingdom and new clandestine churches were established following the Revocation in 1685 and the War of the Camisards. Men and women surprised at secret gatherings were sent to the galleys and prisons. The children of marital unions who had not been blessed by a priest were not considered French. Young girls were kidnapped and shut up in convents. Pastors were punished with death. Antoine Court founded a school for pastoral training in 1730 at Lausanne from which many students would become martyrs. Pastor Durand who preached in Vivarais was hanged in 1732, and Morel-Duvernet was shot to death while attempting to escape from captivity. In 1745 Pastor Roger was hanged at Grenoble; Louis Ranc suffered the same fate the following year.[3]

Beginning in 1755, Protestants imprisoned for their faith in provinces throughout the kingdom obtained their freedom. Often they were freed through the intervention of foreigners or for payment. By 1759 only forty-one galley slaves, whose crime was attending a forbidden assembly or providing hospitality for a pastor, remained on the king's galleys. The city of Toulouse, where in 1532 some of the first Reformed martyrs perished at the stake, shed the last drops of blood for the crime of heresy. One of the most well-known martyrs was Pastor François Rochette, condemned in 1762 and hanged for religious reasons.[4] Passing before the church of Saint-Etienne he pronounced his last words:

> I ask God's forgiveness for all my sins, and I firmly believe that they have been washed away by the blood of Jesus Christ who has redeemed us by a great price. I do not need to ask for forgiveness from the king. I have always honored him as the anointed one of the Lord. I have always been a good and faithful subject. . . . Concerning justice, which I have not offended, I pray that God might forgive my judges.[5]

3. Miquel, *Guerres de religion*, 514.
4. Félice, *Histoire des Protestants* (1), 492–93.
5. Félice, *Histoire des Protestants* (1), 495–96.

The last pastor martyred for his faith was François Charmussy, arrested and beaten in 1771. He died in prison several days later before his court appearance. The last prisoners were released from the king's galleys in 1775. The Huguenots had little reason to express regret over the end of the "Christian monarchy" of Louis XIV and his descendants.[6]

Philosophers, generally critical of Christianity, nonetheless defended Protestants and decried the barbarity directed toward them. Jean-Jacques Rousseau (l. 1712–1778) published *Du Contrat social ou Principes du droit politique* in 1762 in which he declared that man is born free and everywhere bound in shackles. Voltaire (l. 1694–1778) and Rousseau both condemned the obscurantism of the Church, symbolized by the affairs of Jean Calas and Jean-François de la Barre.[7] Voltaire led a struggle to restore the name of Calas, tortured and executed on March 9, 1762, after being falsely accused of killing his son to prevent him from converting to Catholicism. When his widow and children demanded justice, Voltaire and several renowned lawyers argued in the deceased's defense. Exactly three years after his death, his innocence was recognized and his sentence was overturned.[8] Voltaire also came to the defense of Jean-François de la Barre, condemned to death in 1766 for refusing to remove his hat at the passing of a religious procession. The defense was in vain and the nineteen-year-old chevalier was executed, decapitated, his body burned, and for good measure, a banned copy of Voltaire's *Philosophical Dictionary* was added to the flames.[9]

6. Encrevé, *Les protestants*, §171.

7. Dusseau, "L'histoire de la Séparation," 13.

8. Félice, *Histoire des Protestants* (1), 497–99.

9. Monod, *Sécularisation*, 52.

EDICT OF TOLERATION

Louis XVI

The struggle for freedom of religion made progress with the Edict of Toleration, granted by Louis XVI in November 1787 and written for those who did not profess the Catholic religion. It is estimated that "the Protestant population on the eve of the Revolution lay somewhere between 500,000 and 700,000 persons and hence constituted roughly 2 percent of the total population."[10] Protestants were tolerated only in the sense that concessions were made since brutal measures of the past had failed to eliminate them. They were

10. Poland, *Protestantism in France*, 8.

forbidden to form a religious body (article 3), were compelled to respect the Catholic religion and its holy ceremonies (article 5), and were constrained to contribute to the financing of the Catholic Church (article 7). The edict was written in such a way as to prevent Protestants from returning to the situation before the Revocation of the Edict of Nantes when Protestants had been recognized as a religious confession. The Edict of Toleration granted rights only to individuals.[11]

Although the edict offered fewer benefits than the Edict of Nantes, it provided legal existence and civil status to French Protestants, permitted Protestants to legally marry without a Catholic priest, recognized as legitimate the children of Protestant marriages, and allowed rights of inheritance to children from their parents. These were individual freedoms but there was not yet unrestricted freedom of religion.[12] Louis XVI, however, outlined an implicit recognition of one of the fundamental rights found later in the Declaration of Rights. In effect, the king stated that long experience had shown that the rigorous trials imposed on Protestants had been insufficient to convert them to Catholicism and further punishment was useless. The text of the edict disappointed many Protestants. Before the official registration of the edict, the Parliament in Paris made clear that the Catholic religion was the religion of the kingdom with a monopoly on public worship, and Protestants were still denied access to positions in government and education. Despite its uncontestable limitations and the opposition from the Catholic Church, we should not underestimate the importance of this step toward full freedom of religion. It was the dawn of a new era for Protestants. There was tolerance, but there was not yet equality between Protestantism and Catholicism, and the latter remained the official religion of the kingdom.[13]

11. Encrevé, *Les protestants*, §272.
12. Encrevé, *Les protestants*, §171.
13. Encrevé, *Les protestants*, §247.

DECLARATION OF THE RIGHTS OF MAN
AND OF THE CITIZEN

Declaration of the Rights of Man and of the Citizen

The Revolution introduced sweeping changes in France. Among them was the *Declaration of the Rights of Man and of the Citizen*. The Declaration was drafted in the summer of 1789 as part of a project to write a new constitution preceded by a declaration of principles. Article ten recognized the freedom of opinion and declared that no one should be disturbed for their opinions, not even religious ones, as long as the manifestation of these opinions did not disturb the public order established by law. The last part about manifestations of opinions disturbing "the public order established by law" was an addition to the original text and was met with opposition from some members of the National Assembly, particularly the Protestant leader Jean-Paul Rabaut Saint-Étienne (l. 1743–1793), later executed in 1793 during the Reign of Terror. The addition appeared to accord more authority to civil authorities to surveille religions. Despite objections, the majority accepted the proposed restriction. On December 24, 1789, the National Assembly decreed that all French citizens had access to government and military positions.[14] The State introduced legal divorce, abolished religious crimes of blasphemy, heresy, and sorcery, and adopted a revolutionary calendar.[15] In 1795, the separation of church and state was introduced constitutionally for the first time. The arrival of Napoleon Bonaparte would throw these separatist initiatives into confusion when he sought to bring religion into his service. Yet the future would reveal that many people freed from obligatory religious duties and rituals would soon fall away from an organized religion that no longer wielded political power.

Execution of Louis XVI

14. Félice, *Histoire des Protestants* (2), 2–5.

15. CNEF, *Laïcité française*, 13.

REVOLUTION AND THE CATHOLIC CHURCH

The removal of the Catholic Church from public influence and the overthrow of the monarchy were among the objectives of the Revolution. The monarchy had reached its zenith under Louis XIV where the king remained the living symbol of a system in which the Catholic Church was the state religion and among the largest landowners in France. The clergy possessed one-third of the land and were exonerated of all taxes to the State while reaping the benefits.[16] In the early days of the Revolution, Catholic and Reformed Christians co-existed in many communities throughout France. The Revolution, however, became more and more hostile toward the Catholic clergy. The battle for republican values intensified while the Church fought vigorously to reverse the losses suffered under the Revolution. The Church had its defenders and the Counter-Revolution continued the battle for ideas and divided France into two camps. The counter-revolutionaries, many of whom had lost privileges, whose lands were confiscated and titles revoked, sought the restoration of the monarchy. Divisions began in November 1789 when on the proposition of Bishop Talleyrand the Constituent Assembly decreed the sale of church and clergy possessions for the benefit of the nation. Priests and monks were convinced that the objective was the destruction of the Catholic Church, the abolition of religion, and the persecution of Catholics. In the south of France, Catholics turned on Protestants who had nothing to do with the proposed measure against the Catholic Church. Some of the nobility hoped for counter-revolutionary uprisings to regain their lost privileges.[17]

The Civil Constitution of the Clergy in 1790 nationalized French Catholicism and was approved by Louis XVI. The tithe, the Church's principal source of revenue, was eliminated in the name of fiscal justice. The number of bishops was reduced. Priests and bishops were elected by districts and departments respectively and both became civil servants remunerated by the State. Pope Pius VI

16. Félice, *Histoire des Protestants* (1), 12.

17. Félice, *Histoire des Protestants* (2), 9.

(p. 1775–1799) condemned this action and priests were divided between those who swore loyalty to the Republic and those who looked to Rome for guidance.[18] "By November 1793, Notre-Dame Cathedral was re-dedicated to the Cult of Reason, and six months later the Jacobin leader Maximilien Robespierre passed a decree establishing the pantheist Cult of the Supreme Being."[19] In 1794, all exterior manifestations of worship were forbidden, and the Church was confined to the private sphere.

REVOLUTION AND PROTESTANTS

During the summer of 1789, the subject of freedom was at the heart of debates. Protestants had aspired to religious freedom and civil rights since the sixteenth century. We should understand their attachment to the Revolution in light of this history. We saw that after Henry IV signed the compromise of the Edict of Nantes in 1598 to end the Wars of Religion and restore civil peace, Louis XIII and Louis XIV emptied the edict of its substance before its revocation in 1685. They were determined that Protestants should perish and refused to surrender the prerogatives of a monarchy of divine right. Protestants had chosen another religion and had lost any claim to have a part in the kingdom, despite their submission to the monarchy.[20]

The early days of the Revolution saw the first public Protestant assembly for worship in Paris on June 7, 1789.[21] That in itself was a defining moment for French Protestantism and showed the progress that had been made since the sixteenth century. In addition, the National Assembly adopted several texts which manifested the will of the majority of the deputies to permit the reintegration of the Huguenot community into the fabric of French society. Non-Catholics were admitted to all places of employment from

18. Gaillard, "L'invention de la laïcité," 23–24.

19. Roberts, Napoleon, 32.

20. Miquel, Guerres de religion, 515.

21. Encrevé, Les protestants, §547.

which they had been excluded. The Assembly also voted to restitute confiscated property and possessions to the surviving heirs of Huguenot refugees.[22] The Constitution of 1793 guaranteed the free exercise of religion for all French citizens. In practice, however, the Convention arbitrarily reversed this right by decrees harmful to all religious confessions. On September 22, 1793, the Convention replaced the ancient division of the week from seven to ten days (*la décade*) and forced all French people to work Sundays regardless of their religious scruples.[23]

Although the Revolution eventually became hostile in many respects to Christianity, it is no wonder that Protestants initially welcomed the Revolution and a new political order which brought about their emancipation from the intolerance and persecution at the hands of the Catholic Church.[24] With the Declaration of the Rights of Man and the Citizen, they were granted equal rights and freedom of worship. The government offered no opposition to opening places of worship in cities where that had been previously forbidden.[25] Protestants attached themselves to the principles of 1789 and the Revolution and enjoyed the protection of the government until the Terror of 1793 of which they condemned the excesses.

REIGN OF TERROR

Louis XVI was the last king of the Bourbon dynasty before the Revolution. In May 1789 he convened the Third Estate to address the nation's fiscal crisis.[26] The Third Estate created the National Assembly in June to draft a constitution. The king resisted and public dissension grew leading to the storming of the Bastille on July 14.

22. Encrevé, *Les protestants*, §571.

23. Félice, *Histoire des Protestants* (2), 15.

24. Vovelle, *Révolution française*, 22.

25. Montclos, *Histoire religieuse*, 106.

26. The Third Estate (*le tiers-état*) was one of three pre-revolutionary orders (*les trois états*) of the Estates-General along with the nobility and the clergy. The Third Estate represented the majority of French people.

In October the king and his wife Marie Antoinette were forcefully moved from Versailles to Paris under surveillance by the National Guard. They sought to flee the country in June 1791, were arrested

at Varenne, brought back to Paris, and imprisoned. The flight to Varennes proved that the king could not be trusted and increased the public's hatred of the monarchy. The following year France established the First Republic on September 21, 1792, with a National Convention (1792–1795) composed of several competing political parties. The Convention began to root out and destroy foreign and domestic enemies of the Revolution.

Maximilien Robespierre

Execution of Marie Antoinette

The Reign of Terror began in September 1793 and ended with the execution of the radical Maximilien Robespierre in July 1794. Under the direction of the innocuously-named Committee of Public Safety, with Robespierre as a leading member, several hundred thousand French citizens were arrested, thousands were publicly executed and thousands of others were illegally imprisoned in harsh conditions. Louis XVI and Marie Antoinette were executed for treason, on January 21, 1793 and October 16, 1793 respectively.[27] With dictatorial powers, the Committee of Public Safety orchestrated a brutal fight against persons and possessions led by proconsuls who preyed not only on Catholicism but also on Protestantism and Judaism.[28] Several pastors were guillotined for political rather than religious reasons. Among those arrested was Paul Rabaut (l. 1718–1794) who had already witnessed the execution of his oldest son, Rabaut Saint-Étienne, condemned by the revolutionary tribunal for speaking out against the horrific violence and senseless bloodshed. Due to his age and infirmities, Paul Rabaut was led to the citadel at Nîmes on a donkey and incarcerated. After the fall of Robespierre, he was released and died shortly after.[29] During the Terror, many temples, churches, and synagogues were closed and public worship was forbidden. The intensity and duration of a campaign of dechristianization varied according to the regions. Protestants did not lose the freedom of conscience or the freedom of worship as long as it was practiced privately.[30] Following the Terror, from 1794 to 1799, religious life generally took place in a climate of freedom and equality. In some places, the same buildings were used successively by Catholic, Protestant, and revolutionary ceremonies. And for the first time in the history of France, the Catholic religion no longer received state subsidies or more protection than the Protestant religion.[31]

27. Encrevé, *Les protestants*, §702.
28. Montclos, *Histoire religieuse*, 87.
29. Félice, *Histoire des Protestants* (2), 7, 16.
30. Encrevé, "Les huguenots du XIXe siècle," 549.
31. Encrevé, *Les protestants*, §991.

CONCLUSION

The Revolution was not completely beneficial for Protestantism although the established principle of the freedom of religion would permit future progress.[32] Many Protestant pastors and believers, seduced by patriotism or natural religion, readily accepted the worship of the Supreme Being and saw in it the cessation of confessional rivalries.[33] Forty-six percent of Protestant ministers resigned their positions during the Terror and only 68 percent of them returned to ministry in 1794.[34] Protestant churches struggled to rebuild spiritually, and many were characterized by spiritual lukewarmness. Some of the pastors had been trained at the seminary in Lausanne and had come under the influence of Enlightenment philosophy and the rationalism of the day.[35] Yet after three centuries of epic resistance and unimaginable suffering, Protestants finally achieved the longing of their hearts—freedom of conscience.

32. Garrisson, *Histoire des protestants*, 235–37.
33. Encrevé, *Les protestants*, §871.
34. Encrevé, *Les protestants*, §896.
35. Encrevé, *Les protestants*, §920.

CHAPTER 11

Napoleonic Concordat
and Organic Articles

1801–1802

Napoleon Bonaparte

THE REVOLUTION WAS INTERRUPTED by the rise to power of Napoleon Bonaparte in 1799 with the intention to limit the Revolution's chaotic aspects and impose new ideals after his impressive conquests.[1] Napoleon restored the Catholic Church's prestige under the terms of the Concordat of 1801 with Rome, signed on 26 Messidor (July 15, 1801), and formally ratified a few months later. The Organic Articles were added in 1802 and provided state recognition of the Reformed and Lutheran confessions alongside the Catholic Church. The Napoleonic Concordat of 1801 defined France's relationship with the Catholic Church for over one hundred years.[2]

Allegory of the Concordat of 1801

NAPOLEONIC CONCORDAT
AND THE CATHOLIC CHURCH

Napoleon came to power in the coup d'état of 18 Brumaire (November 9, 1799) and toppled the Directory, the government of France

1. Edgar, *La carte protestante*, 49.
2. Félice, *Histoire des Protestants* (2), 19.

during the last four years of the Revolution from 1795 to 1799. He began to reverse many of the gains of the Revolution, initially as First Consul (1799–1804) and then as emperor (1804–1814/15).[3] An alliance with the Catholic Church became a political necessity since many French were still attached to their traditional religion. The State needed the Church to assume tasks, such as education, that the State did not wish or was unable to administer.

Napoleon's Coup d'Etat

Napoleon's arrival to power coincided with the election of Pope Pius VII (p. 1800–1823). Napoleon desired to establish religious peace and Pius desired to restore the unity of the Church. The result was the seventeen articles of the Concordat to define the status of the Catholic Church in France. All church properties

3. Roberts, *Napoleon*, 218.

seized during the Revolution were retained by those who acquired them. The ten-day revolutionary calendar was terminated and Sunday was restored as the first day of the week for rest and worship. The Concordat healed the breach between the Church and the French State caused by the anti-religious policies of the French Revolution.[4]

Pope Pius VII

Napoleon refused the pope's request that Catholicism be declared the state religion. According to the preamble, Catholicism remained "the religion of the great majority of French citizens" with no privileged status. Article one stipulated the free exercise of the Catholic, Apostolic, and Roman religion in France. The First

4. Roberts, *Napoleon*, 272–73.

Consul (Napoleon) had the authority to appoint Catholic bishops (article 5) who swore obedience and loyalty to the government of the French Republic (article 6). Pope Pius VII promised that neither he nor his successors would disturb those who had acquired ecclesiastical possessions (article 13). In turn, the State guaranteed financial assistance for bishops and clergy (article 14).

PROTESTANTS AND THE ORGANIC ARTICLES

The Organic Articles were Napoleon's unilateral appendix to the Concordat promulgated on 18 Germinal (April 7, 1802). They were added to prevent a return to past religious conflict and for the reorganization of the Protestant religion.[5] The State officially recognized the Protestant religion for the first time in the history of France. Through the Organic Articles, Napoleon sought to establish not only the freedom of religion but also the equality of religions.[6] The majority of Protestant pastors welcomed this official recognition. They sacrificed a part of their religious independence and gained salaries from the State. They also no longer had an officially recognized confession of faith and no provision for church synods that had been at the heart of Reformed church government. Decades later the Reformed Church would seek a revision of the Organic Articles to ensure its independence, and the issue of a confession of faith would divide the church.[7]

One section of the Organic Articles provided seventy-seven additional articles for the Catholic Church. Another section addressed the Protestant religion with forty-four articles of regulations, limitations, and restrictions. There were specific regulations for Reformed and Lutheran churches and general regulations for both Protestant confessions, together brought under the protection and surveillance of the State. The first article prohibited ministry in France to all foreigners, which severely hindered evangelical expansion in the country. Article three required pastors to

5. Roberts, *Napoleon*, 274.
6. Encrevé, *Les protestants*, §1452.
7. Félice, *Histoire des Protestants* (2), 21–25.

pray for "the prosperity of the French Republic and for the Consuls," and all seminary professors would be appointed by the First Consul (article 11). Protestants were divided in their views of the Concordat and Organic Articles, which brought churches into the service of the State. The status gained and the stipends granted to the recognized religious confessions under the Concordat were not provided to other confessions. The Napoleonic penal code harshly sanctioned all possibility of gatherings apart from official religious confessions.[8]

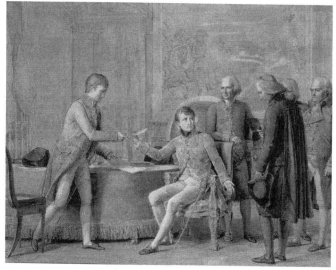

Signature of the Concordat

After over a century of struggle following Louis XIV and the Revocation of the Edict of Nantes in 1685, and despite government control of religious matters, it was not surprising that many Protestants enthusiastically greeted the Concordat and Organic Articles imposed by Napoleon. They limited the authority of the Catholic Church, offered a measure of religious pluralism, and brought religious peace, although there were occasional local exceptions of violence. Protestantism had lost half its population through wars and emigration, and it appeared that its spiritual forces were spent.

8. Carluer, "Liberté de dire," 42–43.

Protestants were given access to most public positions, and pastors became paid employees of the State with an oath of loyalty to the State. Protestant churches were reorganized into consistories tasked with calling pastors to churches with government confirmation. The Emperor created a Protestant Faculty of Theology at Montauban in 1808. In time, some Reformed church leaders came to believe that it was no longer possible to defend the arrangement. They called Reformed believers back to their Reformation roots and the doctrines known as Calvinism.[9]

BOURBON RESTORATION

Louis XVIII

9. Félice, *Histoire des Protestants* (2), 29.

The Bourbon dynasty's restoration under Louis XVIII (r. 1814–1824) followed Napoleon's abdication and first exile in 1814. The Restoration was halted for a brief period when Napoleon escaped from the island of Elba and returned to the throne for one hundred days before his defeat at Waterloo on June 18, 1815. He was exiled a second time to the island of Saint Helena where he died in 1821.[10] Louis XVIII's return from exile was accompanied by a spirit of religious retaliation. He made it known that he did not want to be king of a divided France. The Charter of 1814 established a constitutional monarchy, guaranteed civil liberties (article 3) and religious toleration (article 5), and reestablished Catholicism as the state religion (article 6).[11] The Concordat remained in force with legal protections for Protestants and Jews, but the monarchy and the Catholic Church were once again united. And when Louis XVIII returned to power for the second time in 1815 there was a wave of violence called the White Terror (*Terreur Blanche*) against those suspected of opposing the Restoration—Bonapartists, Republicans, and Protestants. In November, when the government ordered the reopening of a Protestant church in Nîmes, a mob attacked church members, and General Lagarde, sent to reestablish order, was wounded. This led to the issuance of a decree signed by Louis XVIII which stipulated that the attack in Nîmes was an attack on the freedom of religion of non-Catholics guaranteed by the Charter of 1814.[12] France experienced a long and difficult transition toward religious liberty in reshaping public opinion. The practice of evangelization proved difficult for Protestants who were accused of proselytism, taken to court, and had their temples closed and reopened again only after appeals to the government to observe the equality of religions under the law.[13]

To the credit of the Restoration and the Bourbons, from 1817 to 1830 Protestants experienced less intolerance and enjoyed many legal protections during the reigns of Louis XVIII and Charles X

10. Villepin, *Les Cent-Jours*, 11.

11. Félice, *Histoire des Protestants* (2), 31–32.

12. Edgar, *La carte protestante*, 79.

13. Edgar, *La carte protestante*, 82.

(r. 1824–1830). There were Catholic factions who sought to impose constraints on Protestants even to the point of forcing them to decorate the façades of their homes as Catholic processions passed by. Protestants saw these attacks as contrary to the Charter and refused to comply. Toward the end of Charles X's reign some Protestant rights were eroded. At times it seemed as if the freedom of religion did not exist for Protestants outside of their temples.[14] During this period there was also an expansion of Protestant associations—the Society of Religious Treatises in 1821, the Society of Evangelical Missions in 1822, and the Society for the Encouragement of Primary School Instruction in 1829.[15]

Charles X incarnated the sentiment of the *Ancien Régime* and took measures to increase the power of the Catholic Church which was seen as necessary for national stability. In 1821, bishops of the Catholic Church were given authority in religious education in secondary schools, and primary school teachers required a teaching certificate from a bishop. He compensated those who emigrated and lost possessions during the 1789 Revolution and forced into retirement most of the soldiers who had served under Napoleon. When Charles X modified the electoral system to favor keeping nobles in positions of power, the opposition took to the streets and erected barricades. The Revolution of July 1830 forced his abdication and Charles X fled the country. Protestants did not directly participate in the revolution but perhaps viewed with some satisfaction the irony that his path of exile led to a Protestant country, Great Britain. The Chamber of Deputies, sensing the urgent need to fill the royal void, called Louis-Philippe, Duke of Orléans as king (r. 1830–1848).[16]

This period became known as the July Monarchy and the golden age for the French bourgeoisie. The Catholic Church was unenthusiastic about the new regime and for good reason. Louis-Phillippe's eldest daughter Louise married the Protestant king of Belgium in 1832; his second daughter Marie married the Protestant

14. Félice, *Histoire des Protestants* (2), 41–45.

15. Félice, *Histoire des Protestants* (2), 51.

16. Edgar, *La carte protestante*, 51–52.

duke of Wurttemberg in 1837; and the crown prince married the Protestant duchesse Hélène of Mecklenburg-Schwerin. For the first time in the history of France not only was the future queen not required to convert to Catholicism but there was also a double religious ceremony, Catholic and Protestant. If not for Ferdinand-Philippe d'Orléans' accidental death in 1842, he would have been the first French king to have been married by a Protestant pastor and his wife the first Protestant queen.[17]

It is not difficult to understand that Protestants preferred the monarchy of July to the Restoration and they experienced a degree of satisfaction in 1830 with the revised Charter. Under article six, Catholicism was no longer the state religion and was returned to the position of the Concordat as the religion of the majority of French citizens.[18] Protestants continued to advocate for the right to evangelize but were often opposed for what the Catholic Church considered proselytism. The Church acted to prevent Protestants from evangelizing in any commune that did not already have a Protestant community. Acts of intolerance against Protestants took place frequently and included kidnappings, desecration of tombs, and attacks on those distributing religious tracts. Most of these actions were the work of fanatics which the majority of Catholics condemned and the court system often came to the defense of the rights of Protestants.[19] Later in Louis-Philippe's reign, "there was widespread dissatisfaction with the Orleanist government. Catholic discontent centered on the lost battle for freedom in education . . . and the decades long battle for freedom of religion."[20] The kingdom again experienced counter-revolutionary pressures and workers' strikes. Faced with insurrection and fearing a civil war, Louis-Philippe abdicated in February 1848. He was the last king of the Bourbon dynasty.[21]

17. Encrevé, Les protestants, §1723–43.

18. Félice, Histoire des Protestants (2), 58–59.

19. Félice, Histoire des Protestants (2), 62–66.

20. Dougherty, "Parisian Catholic Press," 8.

21. Edgar, La carte protestante, 54.

CONCLUSION

The Concordat and Organic Articles had been a noble attempt at religious pluralism to restore domestic tranquility and prevent a return to open hostility between Catholics and Protestants. They survived for one hundred years to navigate the conflicts between religion and state in France before their abrogation by France's 1905 Law of Separation of Church and State. The nineteenth century would present new challenges for Protestants under the Second Republic, the Second Empire, and the Third Republic. Political events, including the Dreyfus Affair and the increased influence of the Catholic Church, favored the rise of anticlerical Republicanism and the movement toward a secular form of government free from religious entanglements and royalist aspirations.

CHAPTER 12

Protestantism in the Nineteenth Century

THE FEBRUARY REVOLUTION OF 1848 overthrew the July Monarchy, ended the constitutional monarchy, and set the stage for the short-lived Second Republic (1848–1851). Louis-Napoleon Bonaparte (l. 1808–1873), a nephew of Napoleon Bonaparte, was elected as France's first president through universal male suffrage. The new government sought to distinguish itself from the First Republic in abolishing the death penalty for political reasons and affirming its respect for religious freedom. All citizens imprisoned for religious reasons were freed. The application was primarily for Protestants since they were the only ones imprisoned for religious reasons.[1] Neither the Constitution of 1848 nor of 1852 made mention of a state religion or a religion of the majority of French citizens.[2]

The Second Republic ended on December 2, 1851, with a self-staged coup d'état by Louis-Napoleon to dissolve the National Assembly. He declared himself Emperor Napoleon III in 1852 with the support of both the papacy and the majority of French Catholics. During the Second Empire (1852–1870), relations with the Catholic Church became more cordial, with a corresponding loss of religious liberty and the repression of non-concordataire churches.[3] Education was the issue that crystallized the combat

1. Encrevé, Les protestants, §1899.
2. Félice, Histoire des Protestants (2), 82.
3. Pédérzet, Cinquante ans, 132.

133

between the clerical and anticlerical parties in the nineteenth century. In 1850, under the Second Republic, the Law Falloux gave the Catholic Church greater influence in primary schools. The law granted the Church complete liberty to open religious schools and submitted public establishments to religious control. There was a revival of anticlericalism and hostility toward ecclesiastical institutions, and Republicans intensified their efforts for the separation of church and state.[4]

Emperor Napoleon III

4. CNEF, *Laïcité française*, 15.

ORTHODOX AND LIBERAL DIVISIONS

In the early 1800s, a religious awakening (*Réveil*) in French Reformed churches took place in Geneva and France under Moravian and Methodist influences.[5] Many churches had drifted from their Reformation moorings and while the façade of religion remained, the form would have been unrecognizable to their founder. Calls to worship had given way to calls to virtuous living and civic responsibility. The religion of Calvin had progressed from the austerity, moral vigilance, and dogmatism of the first Calvinists to a natural religion, a religion of common sense, a religion deeply in need of a spiritual awakening.[6] The absence of a national synod and doctrinal authority since the Organic Articles of 1802 led to doctrinal dissension between orthodox evangelicals influenced by the *Réveil*, and liberals who departed from confessional orthodoxy. Many faithful pastors sounded the alarm but their voices were largely met with antipathy.[7]

The *Réveil* reaffirmed the great doctrinal emphases of the Reformation—the deity of Christ, salvation by faith in Christ alone, the necessity of the new birth, and the divine inspiration of the Bible. There was a renewed emphasis on evangelization and discussions on the necessity of the separation of church and state. Protestants remained divided in their views of the Concordat and Organic Articles. From 1820 to 1848, independent churches of professing believers were founded and existed alongside concordataire Lutheran and Reformed churches which were divided into orthodox and liberal.[8] The orthodox were committed to the historical, fundamental doctrines of the Christian faith; the liberals had in their ranks those who denied these fundamentals and redefined the gospel in moralistic terms as a way of life.[9]

5. See McNutt, *Calvin Meets Voltaire*, for a scholarly study of Genevan clergy from 1685 to 1798.

6. Maury, *Le Réveil Religieux*, 11–12.

7. Encrevé, *Les protestants*, §2206.

8. Encrevé, *Les protestants*, §2274.

9. Maury, *Le Réveil Religieux*, vi–vii.

The most contentious issue concerned the necessity of a confession of faith which liberals rejected. Many of the orthodox leaders wanted a confession of faith but did not want to divide Reformed churches. Several leaders, among them Pastor Frédéric Monod (l. 1794–1863) and Agénor de Gasparin (l. 1810–1871), maintained the necessity of a confession of faith. After failing in their attempts to persuade others of their conviction, they resigned from their positions and called on others to follow them in organizing an evangelical Reformed church.[10] Monod and de Gasparin and their followers associated with independent evangelical churches and founded the Union of Evangelical Free Churches of France. This union of churches advocated for the separation of church and state and a return to the Confession of La Rochelle. Few followed them in this endeavor, and for the majority of concordataire Protestants, the church contained believers and unbelievers. For the Reformed evangelicals, conversion was necessary to constitute a church.[11] A confession of faith was adopted in 1849 and was clear in its affirmation that their churches would be composed of members who made an explicit and personal profession of faith.[12] The issue of the necessity of a confession of faith continued to divide Reformed churches throughout the 1800s and eventually would lead to new associations of churches and a schism in the Reformed Church in 1879.[13]

In 1859 Protestants celebrated the Jubilee of the first national synod of 1559. They recalled 1559 when Protestants were burned at the stake, the year 1659 when the Edict of Nantes was changed into an Edict of Grace by Cardinal Richelieu before its Revocation in 1685, and the year 1759 when Protestants were semi-tolerated without any legal rights and still subject to persecution. What progress had been made for religious freedom! The freedom and equality of religions were now written in French constitutions. For three hundred years no religious confession, proportionate to its

10. Baty, "Églises évangéliques," 53–67.
11. Fath, Du Ghetto au réseau, 123.
12. Baty, "Églises évangéliques," 294.
13. Félice, Histoire des Protestants (2), 189.

numbers, had counted so many prisoners, martyrs, and exiled. How many families could look back in history and discover their forefathers who were imprisoned or condemned to the galleys, children kidnapped on the authority of the State, entire families disposed of their properties, and others maltreated by the king's *dragons* forcibly lodged in their homes? The Jubilee commission struck a medal to commemorate the event. On one side were the members of the first synod standing in prayer, the Bible in hand. On the other side were the words of Jesus: "Heaven and earth will pass away but my words will not pass away."[14]

THIRD REPUBLIC

The year 1870 was pivotal in the political and religious life of France. On July 18, bishops of the Catholic Church from around the world gathered at Saint Peter's Basilica in Rome to vote their approval of the dogma of the infallibility of the pope. In speaking *ex cathedra*, the pope was preserved from error in faith and practice. With this proclamation, the Church effectively put an end to papal opposition from the Gallican wing of the French Church which favored autonomy from Rome. On July 19, one day after the papal proclamation, France declared war on Prussia. Emperor Napoleon III had already stood against the Prussian war machine and had decisively defeated the armies of Denmark and Austria in 1864 and 1866, respectively. This time France suffered a humiliating defeat in a mere six weeks. One of the ironies of this defeat was that descendants of persecuted and exiled French Huguenots from the previous century were counted among Prussia's military forces. Following the resounding rout of the French army, the emperor abdicated his throne after an uprising in Paris which brought an end to the Second Empire. Louis-Napoleon III was imprisoned by the Prussians and went into exile in England, where he died in 1873. The defeat of the French in 1870 and the constitutional

---

14. Félice, *Histoire des Protestants*, (2) 93–100.

uncertainty provoked by the fall of the Second Empire resulted in a crisis of leadership and conscience.[15]

The end of the Second Empire was followed by the Third Republic (1870–1940). After the uprising and the suppression of the Paris Commune,[16] the Republic entered into a bitter struggle with the Catholic Church in a campaign for the secularization of education and society.[17] The educational laws enacted between 1881 and 1882 under Jules Ferry (l. 1832–1893) attempted to reverse the gains and resurgence of the Catholic Church made under the Bourbons and Napoleon III. The Catholic Church lost influence when it was removed from public schools. Public education became free, compulsory, and secular. Religious instruction was eliminated from the curricula. In 1882, a law was adopted to secularize primary education. To assure confessional neutrality in elementary schools, the law removed all references to God, and moral and civic instruction were separated from religious references.[18] Republicans continued their opposition to the Catholic Church and the return of the monarchy. They firmly believed that the Revolution had snatched the French people from the slavery in which they were held by religion and the monarchy. Both Republicans and religionists tended to focus on the worst aspects of their adversaries. Their mutual hatred prevented them from working together in areas for the common good.[19] Protestants largely aligned with the Republicans in preserving the civil and religious gains of the 1789 Revolution and a diminished Catholic influence. In anti-Protestant attacks of the 1880s, two issues were at the forefront: in political life, France was a Republic and no longer a monarchy; in education, the public school was secular and no longer confessional.[20]

15. Dansette, *Histoire religieuse*, 37.

16. The Paris Commune was a revolutionary government that seized power in Paris for two months in 1871.

17. Encrevé, *Les protestants*, §2987.

18. Machelon, *La laïcité demain*, 17.

19. Dansette, *Histoire religieuse*, 58–64.

20. Encrevé, *Les protestants*, §3001.

The Third Republic witnessed, for the first time in French history, a Protestant influence that had been minimal until this time. As a "small minority swallowed up in a Catholic sea," Protestants had been excluded from national life.[21] They held grudges against both the Catholic Church and the monarchy. They were sometimes persecuted, sometimes tolerated, and mostly voiceless until the Revolution reintegrated Protestantism into the national community. Since religious instruction in the schools was Catholic, Protestants favorably viewed laws secularizing education. They advocated educational reform, the separation of church and state, and social action. It was during the Third Republic that Protestantism achieved the climax of its influence in public life.[22] When the Republicans came to power in the 1879 elections, the Protestant William Waddington (l. 1826–1894) served as Prime Minister and half the members of the Senate and Chamber of Deputies were Protestant, at a time when Protestants were less than two percent of the French population.[23]

During the Third Republic, the Reformed Church held its first general synod in 1872 since the introduction of the Concordat and Organic Articles (1801–1802). The constitution of the Reformed Church written by John Calvin had been accepted by the first national synod in 1559. Since that time divergent theological views threatened to fracture the church. Evangelicals wanted to reassert the grand doctrines of the Reformation, establish a confession of faith, and advance the discussion on the separation of church and state. Liberals opposed the calling of a synod, contested its legitimacy, and called on the government to withhold official ratification of the synod's decisions. The liberal wing found itself in the minority among Reformed churches and protested against what they considered a restoration of the sixteenth-century Reformed Church.[24] The Council of State declared the legality of the general synod. The authority and competence of this assembly were

21. Poland, *Protestantism in France*, 3.

22. Edgar, *La carte protestante*, 79.

23. Encrevé, *Les protestants*, §135.

24. Félice, *Histoire des Protestants* (2), 166.

established and soon after the government authorized the promulgation of its decisions which included the necessity of a confession of faith. The Reformed Church entered legally and definitively into possession of its ancient synodal institutions.[25]

CONCLUSION

The last decades of the nineteenth century witnessed an ongoing struggle between anticlerical, republican forces, loyal to the principles of the 1789 Revolution, and monarchists who sought the return of the union of the Church and monarchy. Protestants sided largely with defenders of the Revolution and opposed any return to an alliance of religious and political powers dominated by the Catholic Church. The Dreyfus Affair in the 1890s saw these issues coalesce in a tragic saga of injustice that contributed to the separation of church and state.

25. Félice, *Histoire des Protestants* (2), 175.

CHAPTER 13

The Dreyfus Affair

1894

THE DREYFUS AFFAIR, OR *L'AFFAIRE* AS it became known, opened a new page in the history of the Third Republic and demonstrated

Captain Alfred Dreyfus

the competing forces at work to either re-establish the monarchy and the Catholic Church in power or to solidify and advance the unfulfilled ideals of the 1789 French Revolution. This event is considered the trigger for the movement which led to the Law of Separation of Churches and the State in 1905.

L'Affaire shook France to its core and led to the widespread reexamination of its republican values. It may be difficult to properly appreciate the importance of *L'Affaire* more than one hundred years after its occurrence. Yet modern historians continue to showcase this as a major contribution to the necessity of the establishment of a secular Republic in which liberty, equality, and fraternity might prevail for all citizens regardless of creed, and where both belief and unbelief would be protected. *L'Affaire* "made possible a coalition of all defenders of the Republic based on anticlericalism. . . . Even after Dreyfus was vindicated, the Affair continued to divide the nation."[1]

CLERICALISM AND ANTICLERICALISM

The Dreyfus Affair is connected to the intensified clerical and anticlerical struggle waged between Catholic and Republican forces following the crushing French defeat in 1870 at the hands of the Prussians. The military loss was a blow to national pride, carried with it the annexation of Alsace-Moselle, and contributed to the low morale of the French military. On one hand, those on the anticlerical, political left ascribed the defeat to the continued influence of the Church in institutions of higher learning. On the other hand, those who supported the Church and the monarchy saw the defeat as a sign of judgment on a nation that had turned from God and the divine right of kings. These two opposing forces would struggle for dominance, and Captain Dreyfus (l. 1859–1935) would become an unwitting pawn to galvanize both sides in the contest for the French form of government. The arrest, trial, exile, exoneration, and reinstatement of Dreyfus would widen the gap between the political left and right. The great majority of Protestants supported Dreyfus in his cause for justice and return from exile. Several pastors including André Gide, Gabriel Monod, and Félix Pécaut, as well as the deans of the two Protestant schools of theology sided with Dreyfus.[2]

1. McManners, *Church and State*, 119.
2. Encrevé, *Les protestants,* §4588.

Alfred Dreyfus Stripped of Rank

Captain Dreyfus was a Jew from Alsace-Lorraine, a long-disputed region that had returned to Prussian control after 1870. He became a convenient scapegoat to assign blame for France's inglorious defeat and revealed the divide between supporters of the Church and supporters of a secular Republic. The incident began with a secret memorandum (*bordereau*) which was discovered in a wastebasket by a cleaning woman and addressed to the German military attaché in the German Embassy in Paris. The memorandum, written in French, contained information on various aspects of the French army—artillery strength, troop placements, and a discussion on obtaining information about a field artillery operating manual. Captain Dreyfus was assigned to an artillery unit, and suspicion fell upon him as the author of the memorandum in part because he was Jewish. He was arrested and accused of treason. The case early on received little interest but was inflamed by elements of the antisemitic press, including the Catholic publication *La Croix* "which called for the expulsion of Jews from France."[3]

ZOLA AND J'ACCUSE

The details of the Dreyfus Affair mesmerized not only the French public but reverberated internationally. In October 1897 the Senate vice-president came to doubt Dreyfus's guilt while newspaper articles continued to treat him as a traitor. Two Protestant newspapers expressed the need for a review of the judicial process and explicitly addressed the antisemitism against Dreyfus from the beginning of the first trial.[4] His accusers attacked the supposed collusion between Protestants and Jews that reinforced the Protestants in their position. French novelist and playwright Émile Zola (l. 1840–1902) issued his famous *J'Accuse* (I accuse) in 1898, an elegant and scathing open letter written to French president Félix Faure (l. 1841–1899). The letter was published in the newspaper *L'Aurore* in defense of Dreyfus. Zola "denounced the framing of Dreyfus by the military hierarchy and constructed the affair as a struggle between liberty and despotism, light and darkness."[5]

3. Begley, *Dreyfus Affair*, 75.
4. Encrevé, *Les protestants,* §4728.
5. Gildea, *Past in French History*, 105.

Dreyfus on Devil's Island

Zola argued that there was no justification for the accusation and described the plot with all the elements of a mystery novel needed to captivate the public. He recounted that Captain Dreyfus was condemned for treason, court-martialed, publicly shamed, stripped of his rank in the courtyard of the École Militaire, and exiled to Devil's Island with the complicity of the military and the Catholic Church. Only when Colonel Sandherr died and was replaced by Colonel Picquart (l. 1854–1914) as head of intelligence did the truth come out about Commander Esterhazy being the real traitor. Even then, the military refused to reopen the investigation for fear that the condemnation of Esterhazy would lead to a review of Dreyfus's judicial process. Picquart was sent out of the country on missions to Tunisia and other places to silence his insistent voice and plea to clear Dreyfus. The general staff could not confess its crime since it would sully the military's reputation, a military still reeling from the defeat in the Franco-Prussian War. Losing face and public scorn were to be avoided at all costs.[6]

J'Accuse: Émile Zola

The condemnation, degradation, and exile of Dreyfus would set in motion his defense by the Republicans. Zola named names beginning with Lieutenant Colonel du Paty de Clam (l. 1853–1916),

6. Zola, "J'accuse…!"

the judicial officer of the affair, who was the most culpable in the affair, and who threatened Dreyfus's wife to remain silent. Zola reproached other military officers for committing judicial errors, for being accomplices in what he considered one of the century's most evil plots, for withholding proof of Dreyfus's innocence, and for committing the crime out of Catholic fervor and biased investigation. He accused three graphologists of fraud in their analysis of documents, charged the war ministry with using the press to influence public opinion, and condemned the first court-martial for introducing secret documents leading to the guilty person's acquittal. The enormous influence of Zola would contribute to the eventual exoneration of Dreyfus and later provide support for the rationale and the defense of the law separating the Catholic Church from the State.

There was the suspicion of underlying religious influences in how *L'Affaire* was conducted. Zola described *L'Affaire* as a crime that hid behind antisemitism and exploited patriotism. According to Zola, General Boisdeffre (l. 1838–1906), head of general staff, reportedly held clerical views. The scandal was viewed as a threat to the survival of the Republic in which Zola feared human rights would die.[7] For his efforts, Zola would be condemned for defamation and experience self-exile in England for a year. However, there was no turning back as the Antidreyfusards and the Dreyfusards staked out their positions. The Antidreyfusards had the support of the Catholic Church and the army. The Dreyfusards had the support of writers, artists, and scientists. The radicals and free thinkers denounced the alliance of the Church and the army. There were more insistent calls for the expulsion of all Jews from France. *L'Affaire* and its eventual resolution, including a second trial in 1899, left France shaken. In the minds of many, "since it was anticlericals, not churchmen, who rescued an innocent man from Devil's Island, the inference was drawn that the Catholics, in the last resort, put expediency before truth and order above justice."[8] This overlooked the fact that some churchmen, though relatively

7. Zola, "J'Accuse…!"
8. McManners, *Church and State*, 120.

few in number, supported Dreyfus and that Colonel Picquart was Catholic. However, it fed the narrative that would continue to pit anticlerical forces against their clerical opponents.[9]

Pardon and Repercussions

Pope Leo XIII (p. 1878–1903) had previously "urged French Catholics to support the Republic, but the effects of the Dreyfus case largely undid his efforts."[10] This policy of rallying Catholics to the Republic may have appeared for a moment to give a chance for a moderate Republic, but in 1898, following the Dreyfus Affair, many Republicans reinforced their anticlerical commitment. "Like another piece of make-believe, but grimmer, the incredibly long-drawn-out Dreyfus Affair aroused passion and prejudice throughout the world. In France, the chain of misdeeds—treason, coercion, perjury, forgery, suicide, and manifest injustice—re-created the cleavage of the 'two Frances,' always reoccurring at critical moments."[11]

At his first trial in 1894, Dreyfus's conviction had been pronounced unanimously. Since then, evidence for his innocence had become overwhelming. Dreyfus was convicted a second time in 1899 but without unanimity among the judges and with extenuating circumstances. He was pardoned after the second court-martial with the consent of President Émile Loubet (l. 1838–1929). The government justified its decision to pardon Dreyfus based on his deteriorating health after five years of exile and imprisonment on Devil's Island. Loubet was considered a traitor and enemy of the Catholic Church. The supporters of Dreyfus would continue their struggle for his full rehabilitation which the pardon did not provide and he was finally reinstated into the army in 1906.[12]

---

9. McManners, *Church and State*, 125.

10. Walker et al, *History of the Christian Church*, 672.

11. Barzun, *From Dawn to Decadence*, 630.

12. Combarieu, *Sept ans à l'Elysée*, 37.

CONCLUSION

The Dreyfus Affair epitomized the conflict between clerical and anticlerical forces. Evangelicals, however, gained a newfound status due to the support of many evangelical leaders for Captain Dreyfus during *L'Affaire*. With the Catholic Church viewed as hostile to the Republic, evangelical Protestants profited from this quarrel with the Catholic Church. Evangelical churches experienced momentum with evangelistic campaigns widely held. Baptist and independent churches were the most active in politics with several influential Protestant senators leading up to 1905. There was an emphasis on morality and economic justice and an unprecedented increase in Protestant evangelization in France.[13] The Dreyfus Affair remains one of the most significant events in French history connected to the separation of church and state discussed in the next two chapters.

13. Fath, *Du Ghetto au* réseau, 128–29.

CHAPTER 14

Law of Associations

1901

THE LAW OF ASSOCIATIONS WAS ADOPTED by the French Parliament on July 3, 1901, in an anticlerical context to limit the influence of Catholic teaching orders and as the first step toward the formal separation of church and state that followed in 1905. Since the majority of French citizens were Catholic, the Catholic Church was especially targeted by this law. Of 16,904 religious teaching institutions, almost 14,000 were closed. All churches were placed under stricter accountability to the State but Protestants generally approved the law since they were less affected by it than the Catholic Church. Pastor Louis Lafon argued that Catholicism and its teaching orders had declared war on free thinking, on every freed conscience, and on the secular State.[1] Protestants, however, were more preoccupied with internal divisions between evangelicals and liberals.[2]

RELIGION AFTER THE FRENCH REVOLUTION

We have seen the religious crisis that occupied France for ten years before Napoleon Bonaparte (l. 1769–1821) came to power

1. Encrevé, *Les protestants*, §5427.
2. Encrevé, *Les protestants*, §5494.

to reverse many of the gains of the French Revolution. By all accounts, Napoleon was a man without strong religious leanings. He recognized, however, that the majority of French people were Roman Catholic and sought to bring the Church under his control for political purposes. An alliance with the Church became a political necessity and the Concordat was signed in 1801 between Napoleon and Pope Pius VII.

After the signing of the Concordat, there were periods when the Church appeared to retrieve its influential place in French society. There were also diplomatic crises, intrigues, and considerable controversies which took place in the last two decades of the nineteenth century concerning the relations between church and state. Conflicts between the Vatican and the French government hardened opposition toward the Church and played into the hands of anticlerical forces who sought the termination of the Concordat. The Law of Associations in 1901 prepared the way for the eventual Law of Separation of Church and State that would end the Concordat in 1905. Of the many individuals who played a part in this drama, several stand out for special mention.

RENÉ WALDECK-ROUSSEAU

In 1899, René Waldeck-Rousseau (l. 1846–1904) was called upon to lead the French government as Council President in the wake of political chaos brought about by the Dreyfus Affair. Waldeck-Rousseau's government lasted three years, during which time he also held the position of Minister of the Interior and Religions. He supported proposals for the separation of church and state and "had seen how the clergy played politics against the Republic."[3] On October 28, 1900, he gave a speech at Toulouse where he outlined a project for the Law of Associations that would require religious teaching orders to request authorization to remain open.[4]

3. McManners, *Church and State*, 127.
4. Bruley, *La séparation*, 77.

René Waldeck-Rousseau

In his speech, Waldeck-Rousseau described himself as a man without a sectarian spirit. He referenced the Concordat which governed the relations between church and state. His main concern was the religious teaching orders of the Catholic Church. Teaching orders had grown in number and militancy and, in his opinion, risked dividing France into two groups by providing religious instruction in their schools. One group would become more democratic, while the other group would remain under the influence of religious dogma that had survived the revolutionary and intellectual movements of the eighteenth century. Waldeck-Rousseau saw the rising influence of the Catholic Church as a powerful rival to the State, an influence that produced an intolerable situation against which all administrative measures had been ineffective. He viewed the proposed Law of Associations as the solution to educational concerns in requiring authorization of teaching orders by the government. He concluded his historic speech by announcing that the Law of Associations would be the departure point of the greatest and freest social evolution and, in addition, the indispensable guarantee of the most necessary rights of modern society. Religious orders could no longer organize or remain in existence without state authorization, and teachers belonging to these teaching orders were not permitted to lead educational institutions.[5]

ÉMILE COMBES

In June 1902, Émile Combes (l. 1835–1921) replaced Waldeck-Rousseau as President of the Council. Neither President Loubet nor his secretary general Abel Combarieu (l. 1856–1944) expressed enthusiasm for Combes. In excerpts from his *Souvenirs*, published to reflect on the political atmosphere of these crucial years of the Third Republic, Combarieu wrote that among the essential policies of Combes's cabinet was the firm application of the recent Law of Associations and upholding of the Concordat.[6]

Combes found in the writings of the famous poet and novelist Anatole France (l. 1844–1924) a defense of his strict application of the Law of Associations. In the preface to Combes's book, *Une compagne laïque*, France evoked the Dreyfus Affair and the anti-semitism supposedly orchestrated by the Catholic Church.[7] He described the agitation that the 1901 law provoked, the surprise and indignation among the clericals at the closure of unauthorized teaching institutions, the organized resistance to the law in Brittany, and the Church's exhortations that led to violence. Parliamentarians claimed that the Catholic Church had constantly violated the Concordat and had pushed the Republican party to its

5. Combarieu, *Sept ans à l'Élysée*, 159.
6. Bruley, *La séparation*, 84.
7. Combes, *Une campagne laïque*, V.

limits, and when the Republican party turned against the Church and requested accountability for the Church's actions, the Church requested upholding the Concordat.[8]

Émile Combes

The policies of Combes did not go uncontested. Combarieu served as an eyewitness to the intrigue and the tensions in the summer of 1902 produced by the application of the law of 1901 and the shutting down of religious establishments. The news that nuns were expelled from unauthorized convents was reported to have grieved President Loubet and his wife who deplored the task

8. Bruley, *La séparation*, 86–87.

undertaken by Combes as damaging for her husband and harmful for France. Combes, however, appeared to have the support of a majority in Parliament, and the president found himself powerless to intervene. Waldeck-Rousseau remarked to the president that Combes was carrying out a thoughtless policy that was contrary to what had been understood at the time the law of 1901 was adopted. He reaffirmed that the object of the law had been to prevent the further multiplication of religious teaching establishments and did not concern existing establishments.[9]

Further opposition to Combes came from the Jewish intellectual Bernard Lazare (l. 1865–1903). In a letter dated August 6, 1902, Lazare expressed his opposition to Combes and the laws enacted in the pretense of educational liberty. He challenged the partisan exploitation of the Dreyfus Affair to tear down the religious teaching orders and the Church. Lazare made it clear that he was not defending the Church against which he had waged combat in the past. Yet he refused to accept either the dogmas formulated by the State or the dogmas of the Church. He insisted on one thing—complete liberty for reason—which did not require force to triumph.[10]

Although Émile Combes severely applied the 1901 Law of Associations, he continued to uphold the Concordat even if the door was left open for its later rescindment. His early support to maintain the Concordat is evident during a debate in January 1903 on state funds allocated to support the concordataire churches under the terms of the Concordat. He believed that the suppression of these funds for churches would bring about confusion. Combes asserted that when he came to power he had promised to support the continuation of the provisions of the Concordat. He confessed that philosophically, and in his political sensibilities on the Left, he wished that free thought supported by reason alone might lead people throughout life, but realized that moment had not yet

9. Combarieu, *Sept ans à l'Élysée,* 210.
10. Bruley, *La séparation,* 91–92.

arrived. Until that time, he needed to postpone the Left's desire for separation of church and state and the repeal of the Concordat.[11]

ÉMILE ZOLA

Émile Zola

Émile Zola's (l. 1840–1902) final novel *Vérité* was published posthumously in 1903 in which he recalled the conflict of the Dreyfus Affair and the struggle against religious schools. He asserted that Rome was the cause of the nation's suffering and its division into two Frances at war with each other. Zola described

---

11. Combes, *Une campagne laïque*, 170.

France as the last of the great Catholic powers who alone had the men, money, and power to impose Catholicism in the world. He contended that Rome chose France as the arena of struggle in its desire to reconquer temporal power and permit it to achieve its secular dream of universal domination. Zola also claimed that under the politics of Pope Leo XIII the Republic was accepted only to be invaded by the Catholic Church. He ascribed fault to the Jesuits and other teaching orders that in thirty years tripled the number of students and expanded their influence throughout the country.[12]

LOUIS MÉJAN

Some believed the Law of Associations prefigured an inevitable separation of church and state. Louis Méjan (l. 1874–1955), son of a Calvinist pastor, was one of the first to see separation on the horizon. He recounted conversations with politicians to whom he expressed his concern that the Law of Associations would lead to the separation of church and state. In a conversation with Henri Brisson (l. 1835–1912) in 1902, one of the founders of the Third Republic, Brisson told Méjan: "Before we might achieve the separation of church and state, France must live through forty years of happiness."[13] On another occasion, in conversation with Charles Dumay, Director of Religious Affairs, a post later occupied by Méjan, Dumay opined that the separation of church and state would be a madness similar to that of a government opening the cages of ferocious beasts in a public place to devour the crowd.[14] Whether the separation was madness or not, France never achieved forty years of happiness, and separation soon become a reality.

12. Zola, *Vérité*, 188.
13. Bruley, *La séparation*, 82.
14. Bruley, *La séparation*, 83.

ALPHONSE AULARD

Alphonse Aulard

The historian Alphonse Aulard (l. 1849–1928), a recognized expert on the French Revolution, expressed his support for a necessary separation in articles published in *La Dépêche de Toulouse* in April 1903. Aulard addressed those on both sides of the issue—those who advocated separation and those who supported the maintenance of the Concordat of 1801. Humorously, he named the two groups respectively *Tant-Mieux* and *Tant-Pis* (So Much the Better and Too Bad) to explain the arguments for and against separation. Tant-Pis accused Combes of seeking reprisals against the pope stemming from a quarrel on the interpretation of the Concordat in the nomination of bishops. Tant-Pis supported the Concordat to have the means to control the Catholic Church with financial support. Tant-Pis also feared that a free church in a free state would soon lead to the Church as a mistress and the State as a slave. Tant-Mieux did not understand how the Church would be freer if the clergy no longer received their salaries from the State and claimed that without state support the Church would no longer have the means to wage war against modern civilization. Tant-Mieux had no fear of the loss of diplomatic relations since the pope advised the clergy to make France a Catholic Republic. Tant-Pis concluded that it would be easier to maintain the Concordat. Tant-Mieux responded that the Concordat was outdated and that the regime needed to be changed in conformity to the principles of the present-day French Republic.[15]

During a speech at the Vatican in November 1903 to counter the aggressive stance of Combes's government, Pope Pius X (p. 1903–1914) inserted himself into the debate. He declared it his duty to intervene in matters of power, justice, and equity. This duty extended both to private and public life, to social and political issues, and not only to those who obey but also to those who command. As supreme head of the Church, the pope desired to maintain good relations with princes and governors. Yet he declared that it was necessary that the Church attend to politics and that no one could separate political matters from faith and morals.[16] Clearly the framers of the Law of Associations believed otherwise. In fact, the law was not directed toward the beliefs and teachings of the Catholic Church but against the politics of some religious orders.[17]

15. Aulard, *Polémique et Histoire*, 161.

16. Bruley, *La séparation*, 117.

17. Encrevé, *Les protestants*, §5750.

CONCLUSION

Georges Clemenceau

Later that same month, statesman Georges Clemenceau (l. 1841–1929) denounced the tyranny of both a secular State and the Catholic Church. The context was debate over whether to repeal the Law Falloux of 1850 enacted during the Second Republic. This law benefited the Catholic Church in granting greater liberty in primary and secondary school education. Clemenceau described Catholics as citizens of a Roman society in submission to a foreign sovereign who were entrenched in revolutionary French society. In his speech, the State was described in these words:

The State, I know well. It has a long history of murder and blood. All the crimes which have taken place in the world—the massacres, the wars, the stakes, the tortures—all have been justified in the interest of the State, for reasons of State. . . . Because I am the enemy of the king, of the emperor and of the pope, I am the enemy of the omnipotent State.[18]

18. Clemenceau, "Discours pour la liberté," 42.

CHAPTER 15

Law of Separation of Church and State

1905

THE 1905 LAW OF SEPARATION OF Church and State was enacted as the climax of decades of nineteenth-century conflict between clerical monarchists and anticlerical Republicans who viewed Christianity as a permanent obstacle to the social development of the Republic. The law ended the 1801 Concordat between Napoleon and the Vatican, disestablished the Catholic Church, and declared state neutrality in religious matters. In French, the law is called the "Law of Separation of *Churches* and the State" since the Reformed, Lutheran, and Jewish confessions were included in the Concordat and Organic Articles. All officially recognized confessions lost their privileged status. Independent Protestant, evangelical churches which arose mid-nineteenth century were not concordataire churches. They benefitted indirectly from the law of 1905 and were placed on equal legal standing with other religious confessions. Most Protestants understood the law as a law of freedom and there was a marked absence of hostility by Protestants toward the law. They announced that they would submit to the law and worked to ensure that the law's modalities did not undermine their ecclesiastical organization.[1]

---

1. Encrevé, *Les protestants,* §5949.

SÉPARATION DE L'ÉGLISE ET DE L'ÉTAT

Separation of Church and the State

PRELUDE TO SEPARATION

At the end of the nineteenth century, the battle for the secularization of France accelerated, and a decisive step needed to be taken. In 1901 the Law of Associations placed the authorization of Catholic teaching orders under the control of the French government. The Catholic Church's influence in education was weakened and the way was prepared for the 1905 Law of Separation of Church and State. The law of 1905, prepared in a passionate climate, was preceded by the rupture of diplomatic relations with the Holy See which rendered the maintenance of the Concordat status quo impossible. The situation of ecclesiastical institutions throughout France was turned upside down. Often presented as an agreement, the law was an act of force that rescinded the 1801 diplomatic convention. In exchange for independence the Catholic Church was not seeking, the law deprived the Church of its patrimony and removed state subsidies for ministerial salaries.[2]

President Émile Loubet

Events in the winter of 1904 contributed to a rupture in relations between France and the Holy See. The rupture originated with a voyage to Rome planned by President Loubet. There had been rumors and discussions on whether the president would request a meeting with Pope Pius X who was more traditional and inflexible than his predecessor Pope Leo XIII. The president initially signaled his intention to request an audience with the pope. Pius, however, tied any proposed visit to the necessity of discussing the expropriation of Vatican lands by the Italian government which led successive popes to consider themselves prisoners in the Vatican. In March 1904 the pope addressed the cardinals at the Vatican and criticized the French government. A stalemate ensued between France and the Vatican that was soon aggravated

2. Machelon, *La laïcité demain*, 19.

by the president's voyage which now excluded any audience with the pope.[3]

King Victor Emmanuel III

The president's voyage to Naples and Rome took place in April 1904 where he met with King Victor Emmanuel III (l. 1869–1947). Together on the palace balcony, they responded to the crowd's acclamation. The Vatican took offense at the presidential rebuff and indicated that a protest would be lodged against the president's visit. Three weeks after President Loubet's voyage to Italy, Rome sent a letter to foreign governments through their diplomatic representatives concerning the French president's visit to Rome. The letter might have remained an affair among diplomats had Jean Jaurès (l. 1859–1914) not obtained a copy which he published in the newspaper *L'Humanité* on May 17, 1904. The public revelation

3. Combarieu, *Sept ans à l'Elysée*, 273.

of the letter resulted in the recall of the French ambassador from the Holy See, the first major step toward the rupture of diplomatic relations. The pope's letter revealed that he considered the French president's trip to Rome and visit with King Victor Emmanuel III a serious incident over which he took great personal offense. He reminded his readers that Catholic heads of state held special ties with the pope and that government leaders should exercise toward him the same respect accorded to sovereigns of non-Catholic States.[4]

Pope Pius X

The pope's criticisms of the French president and accusations of hostility toward the Vatican would not go unanswered. Jaurès contended that the letter was a provocation to both France and Italy. In his view, the pope had not hesitated to accuse the French Republic and its president before other governments. This was considered a declaration of war by the papacy on modern Italy and the French Revolution. As a result, Jaurès envisioned the necessity of breaking diplomatic relations between France and the papacy.

4. Bruley, *La séparation*, 137–38.

He declared that the complete emancipation of France, finally rid of all political interference from the Church, was now a national necessity. Politicians, particularly those of the extreme Left, clamored for the immediate termination of the Concordat following the publication of the pope's letter. The conflict with the Vatican revealed the incompatibility which existed between the Catholic Church and a democratic nation. This incident presented the opportunity to liberate the State from all religious influence.[5]

On August 2, 1904, Jaurès published a speech in *L'Humanité* arguing that democracy and secularization were identical. According to him, democracy assured complete and necessary freedom for all consciences, all beliefs, and all religions. No religious dogma could become the rule and the foundation of social life. In his opinion, democracy did not require a newborn to belong to any confession, did not require citizens to belong to any religion to guarantee their rights, and did not ask the voting citizen to which religion he or she belonged. He concluded that if democracy was founded outside of all religious systems, if democracy was guided without any dogmatic or supernatural intervention, and if democracy expected development only from the progress of conscience and science, then democracy would be secular in its essence and its forms. A corollary to this reasoning was that education must be constituted on secular foundations. Later that month, Jaurès published an article in *La Dépêche du Midi* maintaining that it was time for the problems between church and state to be finally resolved.[6] For the first time, a timeframe was proposed for a vote on separation early in 1905. The separation would not be decided until December 1905, but the direction of the government and the urgency of action became clear.

A speech considered decisive in the movement toward separation was given by Council President Émile Combes in September 1904. He declared that the religious authorities had shredded the Concordat and he did not intend to restore it. His understanding of the political system entailed the subordination of all institutions

5. Jaurès, "La Provocation."
6. Bruley, *La séparation*, 153.

to the supremacy of the republican and secular State, in other words, the complete secularization of society. Combes described the opposition to the Republic from royalists, nationalists, and clericals, the latter considered the most to be feared. The 1901 Law of Associations had been the first step to freeing the nation from religious control. For the past century, according to Combes, the French State and the Church lived under a Concordat regime that never produced its natural and legal effects and had only been an instrument of combat and domination.[7]

The French government warned the Vatican of the serious consequences of continued violations of the Concordat and demanded that the Vatican confirm whether it would submit itself to the obligations of the Concordat. When the government received no response from the Vatican, Combes informed the Vatican that diplomatic relations were broken and expressed his wish that the separation of church and the state might inaugurate a new and lasting era of social harmony in guaranteeing genuine liberty to religious communities under the uncontested sovereignty of the State.[8]

OPPOSITION TO SEPARATION

A preliminary proposal for the separation was adopted by the government's Council of Ministers. In response, Protestant theologian Raoul Allier (l. 1862–1939) wrote a series of articles that had a great impact in shaping public opinion. Protestants viewed the project as harmful to Protestant churches, a project which would result in a new wave of persecution. Two Jewish rabbis weighed in with their perspectives on the proposed document. Rabbi Zadoc Kahn (l. 1839–1905) expressed his reservations about ending the Concordat, fearing that it would threaten national unity. Rabbi J. Lehmann (l. 1843–1917), director of the Jewish seminary, expressed his concern for religious edifices and religious traditions.

---

7. Bruley, *La séparation*, 157–59.

8. Bruley, *La séparation*, 160.

With only one hundred thousand Jewish adherents in France and French territories, the desire was conveyed to continue to live peacefully under current laws as a minority religion.[9]

Albert de Mun

Albert de Mun (l. 1841–1914), an anti-Republican deputy, vigorously opposed the separation of church and state. As a Catholic, he regarded the proposed law as contrary to the teaching of the Catholic Church. As a Frenchman, he deemed the law in opposition to the traditions of the ancient Catholic nation and destined to lead the nation to interior and exterior decline. There was fear that the separation would lead to persecution against the Catholic religion which had already suffered from the forced closure of religious teaching orders. A religious war was envisioned as a consequence of the law, and in the end, France and the Catholic Church would need to enact another treaty. In the

9. Allier, "L'Enquête du Siècle," 267.

meantime, Mun exhorted Catholics to remain firm and to begin preparation for sacrifices required in a separation described as a "mirage of liberty."[10] The bishop of Nancy, Monseigneur Turinaz (l. 1838–1918), explained the reasons for which the Church would fight against the project of separation. The bishop feared the State would take church property without indemnification. He affirmed that the form of government was unimportant to him and that he did not fault the Republic. His opposition was toward governmental decrees and actions done in the name of the Republic.

SUPPORT FOR SEPARATION

Paul Lafargue (l. 1842–1911), the son-in-law of Karl Marx, supported the abrogation of the Concordat and the proposed separation of church and state. He believed that the Catholic Church would be impacted both in its prestige and economically. He refuted the idea that state subsidies for religious institutions and salaries for the clergy were the nation's debt to the clergy for confiscations of property and possessions during the Revolution. Lafargue claimed that it was not the nation but the bourgeoisie which had dismembered and cornered for themselves the lands of the Church and that the revolutionary bourgeoisie, in seizing the possessions of the clergy, had only robbed the robbers. Christianity was described as a constitutional illness that the bourgeoisie had in its blood. He lamented that the revolutionaries of 1789 had pressed on too quickly in their promise to dechristianize France and that the bourgeoisie was victorious.[11]

Anatole France (l. 1844–1924) published *L'Église et la République* in January 1905 at the time Parliament was beginning its deliberations on the project of separation. In chapter eight he raised and responded affirmatively to the question, "Must the State separate from the Church?"[12] It was argued that the progress

10. Mun, *Contre la séparation*, 64.

11. Bruley, *La séparation*, 183–84.

12. France, *L'Église et la République*, 91–100.

of civilization in nations determined a clear distinction between civil and religious spheres. The Concordat was seen as a danger to the State. He related a story from his childhood when he was questioned about his religion for a census. France initially responded that he did not belong to any religion. The census taker prodded him to choose a religion anyway so the form would be complete. When France announced that he was Buddhist, the perplexed census worker replied that there were only three columns to choose from and Buddhism was not among them. For France, that response indicated that the State only recognized three forms of the divine and he regarded as unjust the fact that citizens had to subsidize a religion they did not practice. In his opinion, due to the Concordat, the secular State believed and professed the Catholic, Apostolic, and Roman religion.[13]

SEPARATION VOTED

Émile Combes resigned in January 1905 and was not able to see his project of separation come to term. A new government was formed under Maurice Rouvier (l. 1842–1911) and continued the march toward separation. The commission listened to many views on separation in seeking the most suitable solutions to confer all liberties and independence compatible with the rights of the nation and the preservation of public order. Since the Vatican opposed any reform or changes in the status of the Catholic Church in France, a considerable and often decisive power for action was given to sociologists, Jews, and especially Protestants. Protestants found themselves at the forefront of efforts to fight in the name of all churches. They pursued the task to militate for a law as judicious and as liberal as possible.[14]

On December 6, 1905 Combes, now a senator from Charente-Inférieure, spoke for the democratic Left in expressing their decision to vote for the law as received from the Chamber in the

---

13. France, *L'Église et la République,* 99.
14. Bruley, *La séparation,* 193.

interest of the law's implementation taking effect on January 1, 1906. The Senate proceeded to vote and approved the law by 181 for and 102 against. The Law of Separation was signed by President Loubet on December 9, 1905. Article one stated that the Republic ensured the freedom of conscience and guaranteed the free exercise of religion with restrictions only in the interest of public order. Article two stipulated that the State neither recognized nor subsidized any religion with exceptions for chaplains in public institutions. Subsequent articles dealt with the disposition and distribution of religious properties to associations and the State.[15]

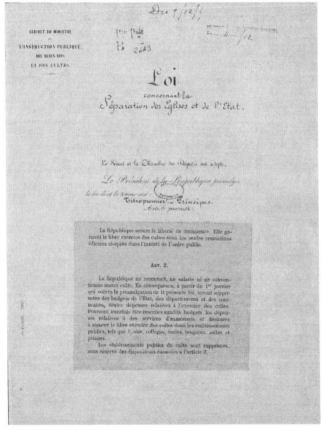

Law of Separation of Churches and the State

15. Bruley, *La séparation*, 299–300.

Although the Law of Separation settled the religious question juridically, religious questions did not go away. The application of the law created unforeseen issues and diverse interpretations and did not end the contentiousness between the Catholic Church and the State. The law was not negotiated with the Catholic Church and was perceived as an aggressive move against the Church. The Catholic Church feared the creation of cultural associations which would escape its control and initially refused to submit to the law. In 1906, "Pope Pius X condemned the separation in two encyclicals, *Vehementer nos* and *Gravissimo.* . . . Further, in condemning modernism in 1907, he condemned the idea of separation of church and state and asserted the legitimacy of church authority which should not be subordinated to civil authority."[16] Protestants largely welcomed the Law of Separation which legally placed them on the same level as the Catholic Church and in 1905 created the Protestant Federation of France (FPF). For Protestants, their future lay with evangelization although their hopes for Protestantism to return to the place of influence experienced in the sixteenth century did not materialize.[17] Owing to historical factors, the Concordat survives today in the region of Alsace-Moselle. These departments were annexed by Germany in 1871 after France's defeat in the Franco-Prussian War and were returned to France following World War I and Germany's defeat in 1918. A condition of their reintegration into France was the continuance of the Concordat.[18]

16. Dougherty, "Parisian Catholic Press," 12.

17. Fath, *Du ghetto au réseau*, 136–37.

18. CNEF, *Laïcité française*, 14.

Church of Saint Pancrace after 1905 Law of Separation

CONCLUSION

Although the twentieth century presented challenges to the Law of Separation, modifications of the law, and new laws to clarify the law of 1905, there was no turning back to the former state of affairs. The battle for a secular State had been won. The Catholic Church would never again share power with the State. Rulers would never again govern by divine right. Dominique de Villepin (l. 1953–), former French Prime Minister (2005–2007), summarizes the importance of the Law of Separation:

> The long path which led to the separation of Church and State flows directly from the inspirational philosophy of the rights of man of 1789. . . . One principle is at the heart of the law of 1905—Liberty. The law established a direct line between secular society and the revolutionary ideals affirmed in the Declaration of the Rights of Man and of the Citizen. No longer would any religion prevail in exercising any influence on state decisions.[19]

19. Villepin, "Une certain idée," 8.

Conclusion

THE ARRIVAL OF THE law of 1905 ended decades of conflict between political and religious powers with the promise of religious freedom and state neutrality toward religions. French society accommodated itself to religious changes in the twentieth century following the disestablishment of concordataire state churches. By 1924, the Catholic Church accepted its new status and adapted accordingly to its diminished prestige, influence, and numbers. The law of 1905 evolved in the twentieth century, particularly between World War I and World War II, and mostly concerning questions of education. The public school's primary purpose remained the formation of young citizens according to republican values.[1]

The law of separation did not lead to the reunification of the Reformed Church as many had hoped. The Protestant Federation of France initially grouped together Reformed, Lutheran, and Free churches, and later some Baptist churches in 1916.[2] After 1905 several distinct groups represented Reformed churches—the orthodox National Union of Evangelical Reformed Churches, the liberal National Union of United Reformed Churches, and the National Union of Reformed Churches positioned between the two others.[3] Also created were unions of Lutheran, Methodist, Baptist, and Independent churches.[4] After WWI efforts intensified to unite separate confessions leading in 1938 to the creation of the French

1. Soppelsa, "De la laïcité," 3.
2. Encrevé, *Les protestants,* §10,953.
3. Encrevé, *Les protestants,* §6130.
4. Encrevé, *Les protestants,* §6153.

Reformed Church (ERF) which included several evangelical and Methodist churches. In 2013 the ERF united with the French Lutheran Church to form the French United Protestant Church (EPUDF) with acceptance of diverse viewpoints.[5]

Many Reformed churches, however, although desiring to manifest the unity of the body of Christ, remained committed to Calvinist and evangelical orthodoxy and created the National Union of Independent Reformed Evangelical Churches. In 2003 the name was changed to the National Union of Protestant Reformed Evangelical Churches of France (UNEPREF).[6] The Union of Evangelical Free Churches (UEEL), created in 1849, adopted a new Declaration of Faith in 1909 at the Synod of Saint-Foy in light of the new political reality under which churches lived.[7] In 1996 the UEEL rejoined the Protestant Federation of France and became a member of the National Council of French Evangelicals (CNEF) in 2011.[8] The influence of historic Reformed churches diminished in the twentieth century and the growth of Protestantism took place mostly among evangelical churches.[9] A 2017 survey by IPSOS confirmed the growth of evangelical Protestants, from 18 percent of all Protestants in 2010 to 26 percent in 2017. Evangelicals are younger than other Protestants with 37 percent under thirty-five years old and also have a higher percentage of regular church attendees.[10]

France has now entered a new era in relations between churches, the State, and society. The relatively homogeneous France of the early twentieth century has been replaced with the pluralistic, heterogeneous France of the twenty-first century. The forces of secularization and pluralism changed the religious landscape of France. With the freedom of religion also came the freedom of irreligion as religion lost influence in an increasingly

5. https://epudf.org/.

6. https://www.unepref.com/.

7. Baty, "Églises évangéliques," 296–99.

8. https://www.ueel.org/notre-histoire/.

9. Encrevé, *Les protestants,* §10,786.

10. Encrevé, *Les protestants,* §10,853.

secular society. The freedom of religion also created a more pluralistic society with multiple religious options. Islam became the second-largest religion in France behind Catholicism. There are tensions that exist in France as secularizing forces push religions further into the private sphere. Religions raise their claims to be heard in a democratic society amid a secular Republic that still bears the strong imprint of Catholicism. In the twenty-first century, France seeks to integrate a larger number of religions from diverse backgrounds into the Republic with its values. France faces the challenge of remaining neutral toward religions that refuse to accept the values of the Republic—liberty, equality, and fraternity.

Whatever the future holds for religion in France, French Protestants are living proof that Christianity will survive. Jesus promised that the gates of hell will not prevail against his church (Matt 16:18). They never have. They never will.

Chronology

1564	Death of Calvin
1568	Edict of Longjumeau ends the second war of religion
1569	Battles of Jarnac and Moncontour
1570	Edict of Saint-Germain ends third war of religion
1571	Confession of Faith of La Rochelle
1572	Marriage of Henry of Navarre to Marguerite of Valois (Aug 18)
1572	Saint Bartholomew's Day massacre (Aug 24)
1573	Edict of Boulogne ends fourth war of religion
1574–1589	Reign of Henry III
1576	Edict of Beaulieu ends fifth war of religion
1577	Treaty of Bergerac ends sixth war of religion
1580	Treaty of Fleix ends seventh war of religion
1585	Edict of Nemours renounces all previous edicts of pacification
1588	Henry III takes refuge at Chartres; Assassination of Henry of Guise
1589	Assassination of Henry III
1593	Henry of Navarre converts to Catholicism
1594	Coronation of Henry IV at Chartres
1595	Henry IV receives papal absolution
1598	Edict of Nantes ends eighth war of religion
1600	Marriage of Henry IV to Marie de Medici
1610	Assassination of Henry IV
1610–1643	Reign of Louis XIII
1628	Fall of La Rochelle
1629	Edict of Grace (Peace of Alès)
1642	Death of Cardinal Richelieu
1643–1715	Reign of Louis XIV
1659	Last Reformed synod at Loudun
1661	Death of Cardinal Mazarin
1679	Peace of Nimègue with European powers
1681	Dragonnades unleashed to force Protestant conversions
1683	Execution of Pastor Isaac Homel

1685	Revocation of the Edict of Nantes (Edict of Fontainebleau)
1689	Return of Claude Brousson and François Vivent to the Cévennes
1698	Execution of Brousson
1692	Death of Vivent
1702–1705	War of the Camisards
1704	Death of Rolland
1705	Execution of Castanet
1710	Death of Abraham Mazel
1715	Death of Louis XIV
1715	Antoine Court and Church of the Desert
1715–1774	Reign of Louis XV
1730–1768	Marie Durand imprisoned in Tower of Constance
1762	Pastor François Rochette and Jean Calas executed
1766	Jean-François de la Barre executed
1774–1792	Reign of Louis XVI
1775	Last galley prisoners released
1787	Edict of Toleration
1789–1799	French Revolution
1789	Declaration of the Rights of Man and of the Citizen; First Protestant assembly in Paris
1790	Civil Constitution of the Clergy
1791	Louis XVI's flight to Varennes
1792	First Republic
1793–1794	Reign of Terror; Cult of Reason
1793	Executions of Louis XVI and Marie Antoinette
1794	Execution of Robespierre
1799	Napoleon Bonaparte's coup d'état
1800s	Religious awakening (Réveil)
1801–1802	Napoleonic Concordat and Organic Articles
1804	First Empire
1814	Abdication of Napoleon, exiled to Elba
1814	Restoration of Bourbon Dynasty under Louis XVIII; Charter of 1814

1815	Napoleon's escape from Elba; Waterloo; Second Restoration of Bourbon Dynasty; White Terror
1821	Death of Napoleon in exile at Saint Helena
1824–1830	Reign of Charles X
1830–1848	Reign of Louis-Philippe; July Monarchy
1848	February Revolution; Abdication of Louis-Philippe
1848	Union of Evangelical Free Churches of France
1848–1851	Second Republic; Election of France's first president, Louis-Napoleon Bonaparte
1852	Second Empire under Emperor Napoleon III
1859	Protestant Jubilee
1870	Franco-Prussian War; End of Second Empire
1870–1940	Third Republic
1872	First Reformed Church synod since Concordat
1879	Republicans come to power
1894	Dreyfus Affair
1901	Law of Associations
1905	Law of Separation of Church and State
1905	Protestant Federation of France

Bibliography

Allier, Raoul. "La Séparation des Églises et de l'État: L'Enquête du Siècle." *Cahiers de la Quinzaine* 1 (1905). https://gallica.bnf.fr/ark:/12148/bpt6k6581797n/f291.item.texteImage.

Armogathe, Jean-Robert, and Philippe Joutard. "Bâville et la guerre des camisards." *Revue d'histoire moderne et contemporaine* (1972) 45–72. https://www.persee.fr/doc/rhmc_0048-8003_1972_num_19_1_2183.

Aulard, Alphonse. *Polémique et Histoire*. Paris: Édouard Cornély, 1904. http://classiques.uqac. ca/classiques/aulard_alphonse/polemique_et_histoire/polemique_et_histoire.html.

Barrett, Matthew, ed. "'The Crux of Genuine Reform." In *Reformation Theology: A Systematic Summary*, 43–63. Wheaton, IL: Crossway, 2017.

Barzun, Jacques. *From Dawn to Decadence*. New York: Harper Collins, 2001.

Baty, Claude. "Les Églises évangéliques libres de France: Leur histoire à travers la genèse et l'évolution de leurs principes jusqu'en 1951." Maîtrise en théologie, Faculté Libre de Théologie Evangélique de Vaux-sur-Seine, 1981.

Begley, Louis. *Why the Dreyfus Affair Matters*. New Haven: Yale University Press, 2010.

Benedict, Philip. "The Huguenot Population of France, 1600–1685: The Demographic Fate and Customs of a Religious Minority." *American Philosophical Society* 81 (1991) 1–164. https://www.jstor.org/stable/1006507.

———. "The Wars of Religion, 1562–1598." In *Renaissance and Reformation France, 1500–1648*, edited by Mack P. Holt, 147–75. New York: Oxford University Press, 2002.

Birnstiel, Eckart. "La conversion des protestants sous le régime de l'Édit de Nantes (1598–1685)." *Religions, pouvoir et violence*, edited by Patrick Cabanel and Michel Bertrand, 93–113. Toulouse: Presses universitaires du Midi, 2004.

Bloch, Jonathan. *La Réforme Protestante, de Luther à Calvin: La réponse aux abus de la religion catholique*. Namur, BE: Lemaitre, 2015.

Bost, Charles. *Histoire des Protestants de France*. 9th ed. Carrières-sous-Poissy, FR: Éditions La Cause, 1996.

———. *Les prédicants protestants des Cévennes et du Bas-Languedoc, 1684–1700.* Paris: Librairie ancienne Honoré Champion, 1912.

Brown, Frederick. *For the Soul of France: Culture Wars in the Age of Dreyfus.* New York: Knopf, 2010.

Bruley, Yves. *1905, la séparation des Églises et de l'État: Les textes fondateurs.* Paris: Éditions Perrin, 2004.

Cabanel, Patrick. *Histoire des protestants en France, XVIe–XXIe siècle.* Paris: Fayard, 2012.

———. "Enchanter, désenchanter l'histoire du Refuge huguenot." *Revue d'histoire du protestantisme* (2017) 409–20. https://www.jstor.org/stable/44850967.

Calvin, Jean. *L'Institution Chrétienne (I and II).* 1555. Reprint, Chicago: Éditions Kerygma, 1978.

Carbonnier-Burkard, Marianne. *La révolte des Camisards.* Rennes: Éditions Ouest-France, 2012.

Carluer, Jean-Yves. "Liberté de dire, liberté de croire: Deux siècles de défi évangélique, 1815–2015." In *Libre de le dire: Fondements et enjeux de la liberté de conscience et d'expression en France,* edited by Louis Schweitzer et al., 35–73. Marpent, FR: BLF Éditions, 2015.

Chamson, André. *Suite camisarde.* Omnibus, 2002.

Clemenceau, George. "Discours pour la liberté." *Cahiers de la Quinzaine* 5 (December 1903) 5–56. https://archive.org/stream/s5cahiersdela quinz01pg#page/n574/ mode/ 1up/ search/ clemenceau.

CNEF. *La Laïcité française: Entre l'idée, l'Histoire, et le droit positif.* Marpent, FR: Éditions BLF, 2013.

Combarieu, Abel. *Sept ans à l'Elysée avec le président Émile Loubet: De l'affaire Dreyfus à la conférence d'Algésiras, 1899–1906.* Paris: Librairie Hachette, 1932.

Combes, Émile. *Une campagne laïque (1902–1903).* Paris: Simonis Empis, 1904.

Daireaux, Luc. "Louis XIV et les protestants normands: Autour de la révocation de l'édit de Nantes." *Bulletin de la Société de l'Histoire du Protestantisme Français* 158 (January–March 2012) 123–32. https://www.jstor.org/stable/24310203.

Dansette, Adrien. *Histoire religieuse de la France contemporaine sous la Troisième République.* Paris: Éditions Flammarion, 1951.

Davis, Stephen M. *The French Huguenots and Wars of Religion: Three Centuries of Resistance for Freedom of Conscience.* Eugene, OR: Wipf & Stock, 2021.

———. *The Rise of French Laïcité: French Secularism from the Reformation to the Twenty-first Century.* Eugene, OR: Pickwick, 2020.

Delumeau, Jean. *Le christianisme va-t-il mourir?* Paris: Hachette Édition, 1977.

De Waele, Michel. "Le cadavre du conspirateur: Peur, colère et défense de la communauté à l'époque de la Saint-Barthélemy." *Revue d'histoire moderne et contemporaine* 64 (January–March 2017) 97–115. http://www.jstor.org/stable/44986654.

Dougherty, Patricia M. "The Parisian Catholic Press and the February 1848 Revolution." *Dominican Scholar* (2005) 1–38.

Dusseau, Joëlle. "L'histoire de la Séparation: Entre permanences et ruptures." *Revue Politique et Parlementaire* 1038 (January–March 2006) 13–22.

Edgar, William. *La Carte Protestante: Les réformés francophones et l'essor de la modernité (1815–1848).* Geneva: Labor et Fides, 1997.

Elton, G. R. *Reformation Europe: 1517–1559.* 2nd ed. Malden, MA: Blackwell, 1999.

Encrevé, André. "Les huguenots du XIXe siècle." *Bulletin de la Société de l'Histoire du Protestantisme Français* 142 (October–December 1996) 547–85. https://www.jstor.org/stable/43498889.

———. *Les protestants et la vie politique française: De la Révolution à nos jours.* Paris: CRNS Éditions, 2020.

Fath, Sébastien. *Du Ghetto au réseau: Le protestantisme évangélique en France, 1800–2005.* Geneva: Labor et Fides, 2005.

Félice, Guillaume de. *Histoire des Protestants de France: 1521–1787.* vols. 1–4. 1880. Reprint. Marseille: Éditions Théotex, 2020.

———. *Histoire des Protestants de France: 1787–1874.* vols. 5–6. 1880. Reprint, Marseille: Éditions Théotex, 2020.

Ferguson, John C. A. "Justification: The Declaration of Righteousness that Shapes Our Ministry." In *Theology for Ministry: How Doctrine Affects Pastoral Life and Practice*, edited by William R. Edwards et al., 217–35. Phillipsburg, NJ: P&R, 2022.

Finocchiaro, Maurice A. *On Trial for Reason: Science, Religion, and Culture in the Galileo Affair.* Oxford, UK: Oxford University Press, 2019.

Foa, Jérémie. "Les droits fragiles: L'insécurité juridique des huguenots au temps des guerres de Religion." *Revue d'histoire moderne et contemporaine* 64 (April–June 2017) 93–108. https://www.jstor.org/stable/26905641.

France, Anatole. *L'Église et la République.* Paris: Éditions Édouard Pelletan, 1905. https://fr.wikisource.org/wiki/Livre:Anatole_France_-_L'Église_et_ la_ République.djvu.

Gaillard, Jean-Michel. "L'invention de la laïcité (1598–1905)." In *1905, la séparation des Églises et de l'État: Les textes fondateurs*, edited by Yves Bruley, 19–36. Paris: Éditions Perrin, 2004.

Garrisson, Janine, ed. *Histoire des protestants en France: De la Réforme à la Révolution.* Toulouse: Éditions Privat, 2001.

Gildea, Robert. *The Past in French History.* New Haven: Yale University Press, 1994.

Giraudier, Fanny. "La rébellion du duc de Bouillon: De la querelle nobiliaire à l'affaire d'État (1602–1606)." *Revue d'histoire du protestantisme* 2 (July–September 2017) 339–56. https://www.jstor.org/stable/44850964.

Glomsrud, Ryan, and Michael S. Horton, eds. *Justified: Modern Reformation Essays on the Doctrine of Justification.* San Diego, CA: Modern Reformation, 2010.

Higdon, Cory. "Martin Luther, Political Theology, and the Contest between Persecution and Tolerance." *JETS* 65 (September 2022) 415–35.

Holland, Tom. *Dominion: How the Christian Revolution Remade the World.* New York: Hachette, 2019.

Holt, Mack P., ed. "The Kingdom of France in the Sixteenth Century." In *Renaissance and Reformation France, 1500–1648,* 5–26. New York: Oxford University Press, 2002.

Janzé, Charles Alfred. *Les Huguenots: Cent ans de persécutions, 1685–1789.* Kindle, 2011.

Jaurès, Jean. "La Provocation." *L'Humanité* (May 17, 1904). https://gallica.bnf.fr/ark:/12148/bpt6k250215f/f1.item.

Joutard, Philippe. "Antoine Court et le désert: La force de l'histoire." *Bulletin de la Société de l'Histoire du Protestantisme Français* (2011) 75–81. https://www.jstor.org/stable/24309921.

Kirschleger, Inès. "'Mon âme est en liberté, et j'ai la paix de la conscience': résistance et spiritualité des femmes du désert." *Revue d'histoire du protestantisme* (2018) 569–79. https://www.jstor.org/stable/45142264.

Krumenacker, Yves. "Marie Durand, une héroïne protestante?" *Clio. Histoire, femmes et sociétés* (2009) 79–98. https://doi.org/10.4000/clio.9389.

Lacava, Marie-José, and Robert Guicharnaud, eds. *L'Édit de Nantes: Sûreté et Education,* edited by Montauban, FR: Société Montalbanaise d'Étude et de Recherche sur le Protestantisme, 1999.

Leconte, Hubert. *Sur les traces de Vaudois des Alpes au Luberon: Parcours historique.* Avignon: Éditions Cardère, 2003.

Lehner, Ulrich L. *The Inner Life of Catholic Reform: From the Council of Trent to the Enlightenment.* New York: Oxford University Press, 2022.

Machelon, Jean-Pierre. *La laïcité demain: Exclure ou Rassembler?* Paris: CNRS Éditions, 2012.

Maira, Daniel. "Luther révolutionnaire: Récupération républicaine d'une légende libérale (1814–1848)." *Revue d'histoire du Protestantisme* 2 (2017) 101–17. http://www.jstor.org/stable/44849194.

Maury, Léon. *Le Réveil Religieux dans l'Église Reformée à Genève et en France: Étude Historique et Dogmatique.* Paris: Librairie Fischbacher, 1892.

McGrath, Alister E. *A Life of John Calvin: A Study in the Shaping of Western Culture.* Oxford: Blackwell, 1990.

———. *Luther's Theology of the Cross: Martin Luther's Theological Breakthrough.* Oxford: Wiley-Blackwell, 1985.

McKim, Donald K. *John Calvin: A Companion to His Life and Theology.* Eugene, OR: Cascade, 2015.

McManners, John. *Church and State in France, 1870–1914.* London: SPCK, 1972.

McNutt, Jennifer Powell. *Calvin Meets Voltaire: The Clergy of Geneva in the Age of Enlightenment, 1685–1798.* Farnham, UK: Ashgate, 2013.

Miquel, Pierre. *Les guerres de religion.* Paris: Fayard, 1980.

Monod, Jean-Claude. *Sécularisation et laïcité*. Paris: Presses Universitaires de France, 2007.

Montclos, Xavier de. *Histoire religieuse de la France*. Paris: Presses Universitaires de France, 1988.

Moorhead, Jonathan. *The Trial of the 16th Century: Calvin & Servetus*. Geanies House, UK: Christian Focus, 2021.

Mun, Albert de. *Contre la séparation*. Paris: Librairie Vve Ch. Poussielgue, 1905. https://archive.org/stream/contrelasparatoomuna#page/n3/mode/2up.

Nouveau Petit Robert de la Langue Française, Le. Paris: Le Robert, 2007.

Pédérzet, J. *Cinquante ans de souvenirs religieux et ecclésiastiques*. Paris: Librairie Fischbacher, 1896. https://archive.org/stream/eglisesreforme esoopede#page/n7/mode/2up.

Poland, Burdette C. *French Protestantism and the French Revolution: A Study in Church and State, Thought and Religion, 1685–1815*. Princeton, NJ: Princeton University Press, 1957.

Pouzet, Philippe. "Les origines lyonnaises de la secte des Vaudois." *Revue d'histoire de l'Église de France* 22 (1936) 5–37. https://www.persee.fr/doc/rhef_0300-9505_1936_num_22_94_2757.

Réveillard, Eugène. *La séparation des Églises et de l'État: Précis historique discours et documents*. Paris: Librairie Fischbacher, 1907.

Roberts, Andrew. *Napoleon: A Life*. New York: Penguin, 2014.

Soppelsa, Jacques. "De la laïcité." *Revue Politique et Parlementaire* 1038 (January–March 2006) 2–5.

Stéphan, Raoul. *L'Épopée huguenote*. Paris: La Colombe, 1945.

Villepin, Dominique de. *Les Cent-Jours ou l'esprit du sacrifice*. Paris: Éditions France Loisirs, 2001.

———. "Une certaine idée de la République." In *1905, la séparation des Églises et de l'État: Les textes fondateurs*, edited by Yves Bruley, 7–18. Paris: Éditions Perrin, 2004.

Walker, Williston, et al. *A History of the Christian Church*. 4th ed. New York: Charles Scribner's Sons, 1985.

Whelan, Ruth. "Enfin Libres!" *Société de l'histoire du protestantisme français* (April–June 2015) 285–93. https://www.jstor.org/stable/44475201.

Zola, Émile. "J'accuse…! Lettre au Président de la République." https://www.atramenta.net/lire/jaccuse/2575/1#oeuvre_page.

———. *Vérité*. Paris: Bibliothèque-Charpentier, 1903. https://archive.org/details/veriteoozola.

Index

189